BETTER JOBS
THROUGH
BETTER SPEECH

About the Author

Harry Shaw is well known as an editor, writer, lecturer, and teacher. For a number of years he was director of the Workshops in Composition at New York University and teacher of classes in advanced writing at Columbia, at both of which institutions he has done graduate work. He has worked with large groups of writers in the Washington Square Writing Center at NYU and has been a lecturer in writers' conferences at Indiana University and the University of Utah and lecturer in, and director of, the Writers' Conference in the Rocky Mountains sponsored by the University of Colorado. In 1969, Mr. Shaw was awarded the honorary degree of Doctor of Letters by Davidson College, his alma mater.

He has been managing editor and editorial director of *Look*, editor at Harper and Brothers, senior editor and vice-president of E. P. Dutton and Co., editor-in-chief of Henry Holt & Co., director of publications for Barnes & Noble, and an editor at W. W. Norton and Company. He is the author of several books in the fields of writing, communication, and literature, among them WRITING AND REWRITING, DICTIONARY OF PROBLEM WORDS AND EXPRESSIONS, TWENTY STEPS TO BETTER WRITING, SAY IT RIGHT, SPELL IT RIGHT, PUNCTUATE IT RIGHT, A COMPLETE COURSE IN FRESHMAN ENGLISH, ERRORS IN ENGLISH, and THE McGRAW-HILL HANDBOOK OF ENGLISH.

BETTER JOBS THROUGH BETTER SPEECH

Harry Shaw

Littlefield, Adams & Company

Copyright © 1979
by
LITTLEFIELD, ADAMS & CO.
81 Adams Drive, Totowa, N.J. 07512

Library of Congress Cataloging in Publication Data

Shaw, Harry, 1905–
    Better jobs through better speech.

    (Littlefield, Adams quality paperbacks ; no. 347)
    1. Oral communication—Popular works. 2. Vocational
guidance. 3. English language—Spoken English.
I. Title.
P95.S5   808.5'1   79–13742
ISBN 0–8226–0347–0

Printed in the United States of America

To the Reader

This book offers a series of practical, pinpointed suggestions for improving everyday speech. It has only two concerns: (1) how people actually talk and (2) how they can improve their speech if they wish to get ahead in their working careers. It deals with practical speech and nothing else. It is *not* a "grammar book." It is *not* a rhetoric. It is *not* a style manual. It is *not* a book on public speaking.

Further comments are needed. First, don't misunderstand the title of this book. Effective speech will help anyone advance in a career, no matter who that person is or what job he or she has. And yet good speech will not replace hard work, reliability, honesty, genuine effort, training, experience, or concentration on the job.

That is, smooth, fluent talk will have no lasting effect unless it is backed up by solid performance. It may be possible to talk yourself into a job or a promotion, but talk alone won't keep the job for you or lead to advancement. Fluent talk neither has nor should have much to do with "talking your way" to a position or a promotion. Effective speaking has little connection with gabby chatter and idle talk. No matter how effective it is, speech can never be a real substitute for effort and on-the-job results.

Second, the book has been prepared and is presented on several levels. This is as it must be, for everyone talks—no matter about what, how much, or how well. If you feel that the education, experience, and cultural opportunities you have had are scanty or weak, then some of the chapters that follow will appear over your head. No matter. If the job you have now seems to require little oral communication with others, parts of this book may seem useless to you.

Again, no matter. You're trying to make up for the past and are looking forward to a more rewarding and responsible job opportunity. Now or later, much if not all of this book will help you. That is, it will help *provided you conscientiously follow its suggestions.*

Also, don't let any difficulty you may have with an accent bother you greatly. Pronunciation *is* important in speech habits, but it is not nearly so significant as are clear thinking and choosing suitable words to form sentences that express to others what you mean. Vagueness and fuzziness will be more damaging to your career than unsuitable pronunciation.

Or let's assume that you have a superior education. Your training and experience are above average. The work you do is on a high level of supervision, control, or direction. If so, some of this book may seem beneath you, too elementary, too simple. Even so, don't carelessly skip over chapters that you think couldn't possibly apply to you. Why? Because years of study and thousands of hours of listening have gone into the preparation of this work. It contains nothing that has not been heard again and again from the lips of top executives, supervisors, foremen, clerks, mechanics, dock hands, truck and taxi drivers, salesmen, homemakers, trainmen, college students, book and magazine editors, authors, school dropouts, and college professors.

Yes, certain chapters that follow will be more important to you than others. Certain of them will fill your immediate needs more than others. But don't assume that any part of this book is beneath you or beyond you. It isn't.

Many happenings in your life will seem more dramatic, satisfying, and exciting than learning to talk clearly and effectively. But such learning is a worthwhile goal and, like all such goals, brings with it many long-lasting rewards.

Contents

CHAPTER 1

Why Speech Is Important to You

You want a job but can't get one. What's the matter? You have a job but want a better one you can't seem to land. You have a really good job but want a bigger pay envelope and more recognition. Why can't you get what you want?

Your lack of success may be due to general business conditions, the state of the national economy. Perhaps business is slow in your neighborhood, city, or region of the country. Possibly there is little demand for your particular abilities and skills. Yet despite these obstacles, you are determined to keep on trying to improve your awareness, to gain more experience. You may even be taking a study course to improve your chances. You try to dress and groom yourself in ways to create a favorable impression. You know that you are not lazy. You have never been accused of being a clock watcher. And still you haven't landed the job, a raise, a promotion. Why?

Have you thought of the way you talk? It tells more about you than any other single activity of your life. What you say and how you say it reveal your intelligence, personality, and even your character more than do the ways you dress, wear your hair, walk, eat, read, or make your living.

Make your living? Many jobs are never landed because of careless, slovenly, inaccurate speech. Many jobs are lost for the same reason. Because of speech weakness, some flaw in the way they express themselves, millions of people stay at the same work level, never advancing to more responsibility and more pay. More time, money, opportunities, and even friendships are

1

lost through thoughtless and unacceptable speech than through any other activity of people's lives.

Don't skip over the comments in the preceding paragraph. Think about them. Apply them to your own work experience. And keep this in mind, too: these remarks are not solely the author's opinions. The personnel managers and directors of four of the largest companies in the United States were asked by the author what part speech played in their evaluations of job applicants and in management's ratings of employees. They were emphatic and unanimous; the most important considerations are always physical appearance and manner of speaking. In separate interviews, each stated that the ability to express oneself clearly, accurately, and concisely is more important than how a person looks and dresses or even that person's training and experience.

Most of the encounters in our lives that really matter are person-to-person, often face-to-face. To others, your speech is *you*. What you say and how yor say it are often all they know about you. Your thoughts may be unusual and even exciting, but if you mumble or ramble or use unacceptable words and expressions or pronounce words differently from ways that are generally accepted you will always make an unfortunate impression on others. There's a lot of truth in the saying "As a man speaks, so is he."

We need to watch our talk because we live in an age of speaking. How much of your working day and leisure time is devoted to conversation and the telephone, how much to television, the radio, tape recorders, and motion pictures? These speech implements are the most widespread and powerful forces now existing for relaxation and for stimulating thought and providing education and entertainment. In the present state of civilization, perhaps 90% of most people's active communication needs are oral.

YOU CAN'T LIVE WITHOUT TALKING

Knowing how to read and write are important accomplishments, yet many people get through life without being able to do either. But communicating with others by some sort of speech signals is *essential* to anyone's actual existence. If you don't believe this, try getting through even one day without speaking or making gestures of any kind. You will wind up hungry, thirsty, too cold or too hot, lost, bored, frustrated, and bewildered.

It is a rare person who does not speak a hundred or a thousand times more often than he or she writes, who does not listen far more often than he reads. Of course words exist in handwritten or printed form, but they come alive only when they are spoken silently (that is, read) and when they are spoken aloud. As the novelist Virginia Woolf once wrote: "Words do not live in a dictionary; they live in the mind."

No one can speak perfectly (anymore than one can read or write perfectly). And yet everyone can learn to speak with greater confidence, fewer mistakes, and more genuine communication if he or she will only study speech habits and practices and give the problem of *talking* the attention it deserves.

You may feel that you have been so culturally deprived, that you are so lacking in formal education, as never to be able to get ahead. Nonsense. It is absurd to think that everyone from a so-called lower socioeconomic class speaks a debased and greatly inferior language. By the age of six, you had made a big investment of time and effort in learning to speak. That the variety of language you use may not seem satisfactory to you, that you recognize the need for improving your speech habits, is what this book is all about.

It is a solid fact that American social standards and business enterprises assume that people will speak a "standard" language. American culture and American business establishments will penalize in many ways, including the pay envelope, those who do not. Language is used as a sorting device in our society.

Standard English, so-called, has nothing to do with character, morality, or aesthetics. And yet no one should ever forget that there are more people with power, money, and jobs to offer who speak standard English than those who do not. Anyone speaking "unacceptably" is often the object of regional, racial, or national prejudice. This is harsh and unfair, an unfortunate truth, but it should be faced.

Four major concerns of speech and speech improvement are (1) pronunciation, (2) use of the voice, (3) vocabulary, and (4) sentence structure.

The chapters that follow, concentrating on these four problems, will alert you to faulty habits of talking, clear up false ideas you may have about acceptable and unacceptable talk, and confirm and strengthen you in those good habits you may have formed.

Before plunging into details, however, you are urged to read the next chapter. It offers "ten commandments" to serve as an overall view of speech improvement and as a constant guide in learning to "say it right" or at least better than you ever have before. If the going seems to get tough for you in later chapters, turn back to Chapter 2. It is a never-failing checkpoint, a guidepost to increased self-confidence in talking and in improvement in the performance of your job.

As you read these ten commandments, pay particular attention to those that you think you violate most often. Some of them will probably not apply to you at all. Two other items to keep in mind: (1) the commandments are not of equal importance. Many speech experts would insist that numbers 2 and 10 are, for example, normally more significant than, say, numbers 3 or 7. (2) The commandments are not listed in specific order of importance, largely because what may be of most significance to you and the way you talk may not apply to someone else. But if you feel that you can keep only one of these rules, make it number 10. This commandment applies to everyone at all times. Further, it is the one that most people violate most often.

CHAPTER 2

Keep These Ten Commandments

Improving speech is a lifelong occupation at which no one ever fully succeeds. This difficult task may seem clearer—although not more simple—if the major steps involved are separated, outlined, and explained. That is what this short chapter tries to do.

The basic steps in improving your speech are listed here in the form of commandments. Each of these ten decrees is within the capacity of anyone free from major physical defects in one's speaking apparatus. If you can keep any *one* of these commandments better than you have been doing, you will have taken a big step forward. If you can keep any *five* of them, you are an above-average speaker. Each requires work, but each can be rewarding. Don't get discouraged. Do you know anyone who doesn't have trouble with *the* Ten Commandments?

1. *Pronounce words carefully.*

Some errors in pronouncing words are caused by carelessness and haste. Others are caused by ignorance, unfamiliarity with the language, a faulty ear, and an inadequate vocabulary. Talk deserves much more care and attention than it usually gets. Treat it with respect. *Words are priceless.*

2. *Speak to be heard.*

If something deserves to be said, it deserves to be heard. Don't shout, but don't mumble and swallow your words. *Say, don't slur.*

3. *Look alive.*

If the interest you have in what you're saying is shown by a lively, vigorous manner of talking, you'll arouse interest in your listener. If your speech is dull and lifeless, you'll soon lose your audience. Your speech is you. *Be sharp, look sharp, talk sharp.*

4. *Take your time.*

Your tongue is slower than your mind, but it's much quicker than your listener's ears. Many people—perhaps you included —speak too rapidly, drop syllables, slur words, and run thoughts together. Pauses in talk can be as effective as words themselves. Let people's ears and minds catch up to what you're saying. Speech that is slow and dragging can be tiresome, but it can be understood. Rapid speech is both tiring *and* confusing. *Slow down.*

5. *Be concise.*

Most statements of any kind are wordy. Each of us frequently repeats an idea in the same or similar words—and then says it again. Talk should not be clipped and abrupt, but it should be economical. *Make it snappy.*

6. *Be specific.*

Much of what we say is not clear in our minds and therefore is unclear in the minds of our hearers. Even when we have a good idea of what we wish to say, we don't use the exact and concrete words that would express what we think we want to get across to others. Make your point clearly. *Don't be vague.*

7. *Be original.*

It's impossible for any of us to conceive of an entirely new idea or to express an old one in completely fresh language. And yet the single greatest error in "saying it right" is the use of wornout, trite, tired expressions that have lost whatever freshness and appeal they originally had. If your talk is like that of everyone else, it is filled with trite phrases, with conversational tags and fillers that add nothing but words, words, words. One reason conversation is so boring to many people is that they know not only what will be talked about but even the very words and expressions that will be trotted out again and again. *Don't be a rubber stamp.*

8. *Vary your approach.*

The primary requirement of effective talk is that it communicate, that it give the listener a clear picture of what the speaker has in mind. But clear communication depends upon who is talking to whom. At times, talk should be racy and informal, as when two close friends are alone together. At other times, it should be more careful, deliberate, and formal, as when one is talking with an important company official or community leader. The tone of your voice and your choice of words should vary from situation to situation and person to person. *Shift gears.*

9. *Learn to listen.*

Talk should usually be a two-way street. It is always tactful and courteous to listen to others. (It's also good business when you're talking with a superior at the place you work.) Not only that: listening is the best way known to man for gathering facts, getting ideas, and improving speech. How did each of us learn to talk in the first place? *Put your ears on stems.*

10. *Have something to say.*

With rare exceptions, people tend to talk more—and say less—than they should. Speech is only the faculty, or power, of speaking. The ability to talk is one thing; to think and to feel are two others. The great Dutch philosopher, Spinoza, once remarked that mankind would be happier if the power in men to be silent were the same as that to speak; that "men govern nothing with more difficulty than their tongues." An English writer, John Ruskin, once commented that "hundreds can talk for one who can think." It was a wise person who, when called upon at a meeting, said that it would be better for him to keep quiet and have some people think him stupid than to open his mouth and thus remove all possible doubt. *Think first, talk second.*

Conversation is but carving.
Give no more to every guest
Than he's able to digest.
Give him always of the prime,
And but a little at a time.
Carve to all but just enough,
Let them neither starve nor stuff.
And that you may have your due,
Let your neighbor carve for you.
                    Jonathan Swift

CHAPTER 3

What Pronunciation Is and Does

The act of making the sounds of speech must be the direct, immediate, and constant concern of everyone who wishes to "say it right." It is also a matter of prime importance to anyone wishing to advance in one's work or profession and to live a richer, fuller life. Because pronunciation is important, we should get straight some facts about what this widespread, everyday activity really is—and isn't.

One notion that many people have—and it's a faulty one—is that pronunciation is the single most important concern of effective talk. It's important, all right, and it does have a significant effect on good speech. But pronunciation of itself is not nearly so important as how one selects and uses words themselves, one's straight or crooked thinking, tone of voice, and general manner of speaking. Several chapters in this book try hard to make this point clear.

Still other ideas about pronunciation deserve inspection.

EVERYONE SPEAKS HIS OWN LANGUAGE

Even if one wished to, it would be impossible for him or her to speak *the* English language or even "American English." Everyone makes speech sounds related to a specific locality, individual background, and particular social group. Everyone learns and usually hangs on to certain speech patterns that are uniquely his or her own, patterns derived from family members, place of birth, the locality or localities in which one grew up, schools attended, acquaintances, occupation, hobbies, and recreations. That is, no such thing as total agreement in pronunciation is possible because every speaker of a language (English, American, Italian, German, French, Spanish, Russian, or whatnot) employs his or her own dialect. Every pronouncer of words in no matter what language has a speech pattern peculiar to him at a specific period of his life.

One's individual speech pattern is known as one's *idiolect,* one's unique way of forming the sounds of speech. If you are accused of speaking with a dialect, you can reply, "Of course I do. Everyone does." To the expert, the speech sounds of no two persons are, or ever can be, identical.

NO SINGLE PRONUNCIATION STANDARD EXISTS

With many millions of idiolects for the English language (or any other language) in daily use, no way of sounding a given word can be said to be its *only correct* pronunciation. True, nearly everyone pronounces more than 90 percent of all words in general use in about the same way, so nearly the same that the pronunciation can be called identical. And yet a trained ear would detect differences. Also, even if pronunciations of individual words seem alike, they would change and shift as they appeared in connected speech (talk, that is) because people speak at different rates and with differing emphasis on specific words.

The differing speech patterns of sections of the United States involve color more than substance, so that communication between speakers in different areas creates no real problem. But individual systems of pronunciation can and do exist throughout the country, no one of which can flatly be called "standard" or "universal" or "correct."

WHAT IS CORRECT PRONUNCIATION?

The only accurate answer to this question is that the pronunciation of any word or phrase is correct if it is one used by a majority of educated, cultivated speakers under similar sets of circumstances in a particular major speech area. This definition suggests that *more than one* "correct" pronunciation exists for many words. Such an answer may seem vague, but it is the only honest, sensible answer possible. It is a fixed belief of all experts on pronunciation, including the makers of dictionaries, that the one and only test for correctness is *usage*. Of no significance in determining "correct" or "good" pronunciations are rules, tradition, spelling, or word derivation. We have no national academy to determine matters of pronunciation. You should think of pronunciation as being acceptable or unacceptable, in good usage or not—never as "correct" or "incorrect."

ISN'T A DICTIONARY AN AUTHORITY?

No reliable dictionary published within recent decades attempts to dictate what "correct" pronunciation is or should be. Only to the extent that makers of a dictionary are considered accurate and unbiased recorders and interpreters of usage can their work be considered authoritative. A good dictionary tries to provide an authentic description of pronunciation usage; it will *never* flatly state that such-and-such a pronunciation is "right" or "wrong."

The attitude of competent dictionary makers is expressed in this statement by Dr. Daniel Jones, author of *The Pronunciation of English* and an eminent former professor of phonetics (the study of speech sounds and their production, transmission, and reception):

> It is useful that descriptions of existing pronunciation should be recorded, but I no longer feel disposed to recommend any particular forms of pronunciation . . . or to condemn others. It must, in my view, be left to individual English-speaking persons to decide whether they should speak in the manner that comes to them naturally or whether they should alter their speech in any way.

We should learn, and never forget, that the so-called authority of a dictionary derives from the speech and writing of a community of what has been termed "effective" citizens. As

Professor Cabell Greet, a recognized authority and a former consultant on pronunciation to a large radio and television network, has said:

> Without seeking to impair any citizen's right to be his own professor of English, we the makers of dictionaries look for what is national, contemporary, and reputable. This is our standard of correctness.

WHY, THEN, STUDY PRONUNCIATION AT ALL?

Every speaker has his own idiolect and cannot attain a fixed standard of pronunciation even if he tries. Furthermore, no rigid standard exists. Finally, not even the dictionary, any dictionary, either is, or claims to be, a final authority. So why bother about pronunciation? What's all the fuss about? Why shouldn't everyone pronounce words in whatever way comes naturally?

The statements made and questions raised in preceding paragraphs lead us back to the remark made earlier that the speaker of English should not be so much concerned about his pronunciation as about his choice and use of words. The reason is simple: diction involves hundreds of problems for every one caused by pronunciation. That is, choosing and using the words of everyday speech is often difficult; pronouncing these same words is comparatively simple.

We use remarkably few different words in ordinary speech, and the overwhelming majority of them cause no pronunciation problems whatever. It may be both startling and reassuring to learn that only twelve simple words account for about 25 percent of everything spoken and written in English. The dozen most used words in English are *a, and, he, I, in, it, is, of, that, the, to,* and *was.* These twelve and thirty-eight more (a total of fifty words) make up half of the running total in all English speech and writing. If you increase the number to the thousand most common words in English, you will account for 80 percent of all words everyone uses in speaking and writing and comes across in reading.

You may be inclined to doubt these statements, but they are

substantiated by the word count contained in *The Teacher's Word Book of 30,000 Words*, prepared under the direction of two outstanding scholars, Edward L. Thorndike and Irving Lorge. Other experts fully accept the findings of Thorndike and Lorge, although the actual word count may differ depending upon whether conversation is face-to-face or over the telephone. In a careful study by the Bell System (American Telephone and Telegraph), the most often used words were found to be *a, I, is, it, on, that, the, you,* and *to.*

If only one thousand different words appear in some 80 percent of all the expressions that one says, hears, writes, and reads, it follows that the task of learning to pronounce that small number should be fairly simple. And yet the problem is even more elementary: almost none of the thousand words creates a pronunciation difficulty for the ordinary speaker.

In a running count of millions of words used by speakers and writers of English, the words *a, and, of, the,* and *to* will appear more than a hundred thousand times; *he, I, in, it, is, that,* and *was* will appear more than fifty thousand times. None of these words is a pronunciation demon, nor indeed are many of the 620 words appearing more than one thousand times in the same word count. For proof of this statement, note the thirty-eight most often used words beginning with the letter *a:*

A

about	almost	any
according	alone	anything
across	along	appear
act	already	are
action	also	arm
add	always	army
after	am	around
afternoon	American	art
again	among	as
against	an	ask
age	and	at
ago	another	away
all	answer	

Do you find any hard-to-pronounce words in this list? Perhaps someone may say *"acrost"* (acrossed) instead of "uh KRAWS" or "uh KROS"; in careless or rapid speech, some might drop the final "g" in *"according."* The entire list, however, is so simple that no ordinary speaker should be concerned about pronunciation.

Just so you will not think that the list is "rigged" with words starting with *a*, see whether the following *b*, *n*, and *u* words used most often are any more difficult.

B

baby	began	book
back	begin	both
bad	behind	boy
bank	being	bring
battle	believe	British
be	best	brought
became	better	brown
because	between	building
become	big	built
bed	bill	business
beer	black	but
before	body	by

N

name	never	nor
nation	new	north
national	news	not
nature	New York	note
near	next	nothing
necessary	night	now
need	no	number

U

uncle	United States	upon
under	until	us
understand	up	use

That only one thousand make up 80 percent of all the words used does not mean that in any particular conversation those words would appear in exactly that percentage. Nor does this fact have any bearing upon two others: (1) some of the remaining 20 percent do involve problems in pronunciation; (2) the actual words comprising this remaining 20 percent vary widely with each user. And yet it helps to know that, roughly speaking, 80 percent of all the words most commonly used present no pronunciation problems at all.

Your best plan of attack on pronunciation is to concentrate only on those words in the remaining 20 percent that you do use and that do cause trouble. No one can accurately state precisely what your problems in pronunciation may be. But it has been found that most difficulties are caused by:

1. Dropped letters

Even well-informed, educated speakers often drop vowels or consonants that should be sounded in pronouncing everyday words. Check your speech: do you mispronounce any of the following words?

asked (not *ast*)
auxiliary (not *auxilary*)
awkward (not *awkard*)
beneficial (not *benefical*)
candidate (not *canidate*)
criticism (not *critcism*)
civilian (not *civilan*)
convenient (not *convenent*)
doing (not *doin*)
eating (not *eatin*)
familiar (not *familar*)
genial (not *genal*)
genius (not *genus*)
government (not *goverment*)
identity (not *idenity*)

kept (not *kep*)
laboratory (not *labortory*)
length (not *lenth*)
library (not *liberry*)
miniature (not *minature*)
partner (not *pardner*)
quantity (not *quanity*)
reading (not *readin*)
supposed (not *suppose*)
talking (not *talkin*)
temperament (not *temper-ment*)
tentative (not *tenative*)
width (not *with*)
working (not *workin*)

2. Added letters

In everyday conversation it is all too easy to add letters where they are not wanted or needed. Many people carelessly mispronounce words for this reason.

burglar (not *burgular*)   film (not *fillum*)
chimney (not *chimeney*)   Henry (not *Henery*)
electoral (not *electorial*)   lightning (not *lightening*)
elm (not *ellum*)   pamphlet (not *pamphalet*)
entrance (not *enterance*)   translate (not *transalate*)

3. Changing positions of letters

Any word is likely to be mispronounced if its letters are transposed or otherwise confused:

irrelevant (not *irrevalent*)   poem (not *pome*)
perhaps (not *prehaps*)   professor (not *perfessor*)
perversely (not *preversely*)   strategic (not *stragetic*)

4. Shifty accents

In words of more than one syllable, one syllable is usually pronounced (sounded, accented) more strongly or loudly than others. In some words, such as *adult, harass,* and *romance,* either syllable may be accented, but the pronunciation of many words requires you to make a choice:

COMment, not *comMENT*   PREFerable, not *preFERable*
DEFicit, not *defiCIT*   REPutable, not *rePUTable*
IMpotent, not *imPOtent*   REVocable, not *reVOCable*
INfamous, not *inFAMous*   THEater, not *theAter*

At the end of the next chapter you will find a list of words that illustrate these four common causes of mispronunciations. Study it carefully, referring, as needed, to the comments that have just been made.

CHAPTER 4

How to Tackle Pronunciation

If you have a good ear and spend considerable time listening to speakers in person and on radio and television, you can learn the pronunciation of many troublesome words. This method of learning by ear has several flaws, however, among which two may be mentioned: (1) not every effective speaker (including broadcasters and telecasters) is trustworthy in pronunciation; (2) in any particular conversation, speech, or broadcast, you may not hear the words you wish and need to learn to pronounce.

The surest, most economical way to learn to "pronounce it right" is to consult your dictionary *when the need arises*. Remember: Do not worry about the pronunciation of any word until you read it, hear it, or feel the need for it in your own speech.

What such words will be must vary from person to person. No two people have the same vocabulary, just as no two people have the same fingerprints. No two people make the same demands on language because no two can have the same audience or the same things to say. As one trying to better your pronunciation, you should make your own lists of trouble spots. Looking up words as you need to and entering them after a period of time in your own workbook in alphabetical order (or some other order that appeals to you) is the most efficient way to improve pronunciation.

Here, for instance, is the record of one person who in one

week found that she had heard or read a dozen words beginning with *d*, about the pronunciation of which she was doubtful:

dais	detour
data	diffuse
debris	diphtheria
decorous	divan
dereliction	duress
despicable	dysentery

Any list of *d* words you would make would differ from this one for several reasons: you would not come across the same words in reading or listening; you would have no problem with the pronunciation of some of them; you would run across other words that would raise problems; not all the words on this list would be those that you now need or expect a use for.

The point is that you should note the words you do need, study them carefully in your dictionary, and record them in a notebook with their correct spelling, meanings, and standard pronunciation (s).

HOW SHOULD I USE MY DICTIONARY IN LEARNING PRONUNCIATION?

Every modern American dictionary presents its own system of recording pronunciation. Your first move should be to find out about that system. Read the essay on pronunciation included in the front matter (first pages) of your dictionary; every reliable dictionary contains such an article. Study the full pronunciation key provided on the inside of the front or back covers of your book, or in both places. Examine the pronunciation key appearing at the bottom of each page, or every other page, of your dictionary. Only after you have taken these steps are you in a position really to use your dictionary as a guide in pronunciation.

Pronunciation, as you already know and as your dictionary will again tell you, depends upon the *sound* given to alphabetical letters or letter combinations and upon *accent* of emphasized syllables.

Dictionary-makers have had to make up systems for representing sounds because only twenty-six letters exist to represent some 250 common spellings of sounds. The best-known set of symbols for the sounds of language is the International Phonetic Alphabet (IPA). This alphabet, applicable to many languages, including English, is accurate, but the ordinary speaker will find it hard to follow.

Your most sensible approach is to study the "pronunciation word" that appears in parentheses immediately after an entry word. It is a respelling of the word, giving the sounds of vowels and consonants by syllables, according to the pronunciation key that your dictionary has adopted. (Every dictionary compiler has chosen anywhere from forty to sixty symbols that he thinks adequate to explain problems in pronunciation.) Study the key in your dictionary to find out the various sounds of letters and letter combinations as indicated in sample words.

As an indication of the kinds of information provided about pronunciation in your dictionary, see how it represents the varied sounds of, say, the letter "o." You will find that the sounds of "o" are indicated by some or all of these symbols:

o—as in *odd, hot, lot, ox*
ō—as in *go, open, over, no*
ô—as in *order, horn, ought*
ŏŏ—as in *took, book, look*
ōō—as in *pool, ooze, boot, too*

Each of the signs (symbols appearing with words in a pronunciation key is a kind of diacritical mark. (The word *diacritical* comes from a Greek term meaning "capable of distinguishing," "distinctive.") Still other signs, or points, are occasionally added to letters to indicate a particular sound value. Among these are the *"circumflex"* (raison d'être); the *"tilde"* (cañon); *"umlaut"* (schön), and the *"cedilla"* (façade). Some dictionaries supply these and other diacritical marks with individual words; other dictionaries provide a separate "foreign sounds" key. All diacritical marks are inexact in suggesting the reproduction of sounds, but their use is one further example of the pains dictionary makers have taken in trying to provide a faithful record of the sounds of language.

The matter of stress, or accent, is less involved than the pronunciation of sounds. But it is important. Examine the method your dictionary employs for indicating where accents fall in given entries. Some dictionaries provide both accent marks and syllabication periods (dots) in the entry word. Others use only dots to indicate syllabication in the entry word and insert accent marks in the "pronunciation word." Learn the methods your dictionary has provided for indicating heavy (primary) stress and less heavy (secondary) stress. Whatever devices your dictionary uses are made fully clear in an article at the front of the book.

If English is not your native language, pay particular attention to accents. English is an *accented* language, and the rhythm of speech quickly indicates one's ease and familiarity with a language.

When two or more pronunciations of any entry are provided —that is, when sounds or accents are indicated differently—the pronunciation more generally used may or may not be given first. One dictionary shows first the pronunciation its makers consider the one most widespread in "general American" usage. Another dictionary lists first the pronunciation most prevalent in ʼEastern speech (along the North Atlantic seaboard). Any pronunciation shown is "standard," although some dictionaries do make a distinction by preceding a given pronunciation with the word "also" or by giving some indication of regional usage.

Pronunciation, the sound system, of language, is important, although less so for the average speaker than diction and what is broadly called grammar. And yet the sound system of language really *is* "the grammar of speech." Although the problem of pronunciation is not great for many speakers in their daily use of language, it should not be overlooked. Every user of language will find gaps in his knowledge when he encounters certain words and will be doubtful about pronunciation. When this situation occurs, one should pull out one's dictionary.

Comfort yourself with knowing that the one thousand words appearing most often in your speaking, hearing, writing, and reading—the words that make up 80 percent of all the words encountered—present few problems in pronunciation. Further simplifying pronunciation is that only 9,000 additional words (the next most frequently occurring ones) account for 18 percent of *all* words spoken, heard, written, or read. That is, only ten thousand words comprise 98 percent of all expressions regularly used. After the first ten thousand, pronunciation demons *do* appear more often. However, words in the 10,001–20,000 frequency group appear less than one-twelfth as often as those in the first ten thousand. Those in the 20,001–30,000 frequency group appear on an average only one two-hundredths as often as words in the most common ten thousand. In short, errors in pronunciation do occur, but they appear infrequently because of rare use and because few words are involved.

WHAT IS MY PARTICULAR PROBLEM WITH PRONUNCIATION?

Assuming that you have no serious impediment in speech or hearing, whatever difficulties you encounter with pronunciation probably arise from three causes: (1) you do not systematically and carefully study in your dictionary the pronunciation of words you need in your vocabulary; (2) you speak in a careless, slovenly manner; (3) English is not your native language.

No matter how cultivated and knowledgeable you are as a user of language, it is likely that on occasion you pronounce words in a hurried, careless, ignorant, or slovenly fashion. No one is always on his best behavior in pronunciation any more than he is in any other activity of his life. Each of us pronounces some words in one way when we are actually listening to what we are saying *and* when we say the words alone. We may sound quite differently when we use these same words in ordinary conversation.

Now, few people are so precise as to wish always to speak in a formal way. Nearly everyone will agree that stuffy and stilted conversation is less pleasant, less desirable, than the give-and-take of friendly communication. The danger is always present, however, that if we engage too often in slovenly, slurred, and imprecise pronunciation, we may find it difficult to pronounce in standard fashion when we really need to.

In the speech of even educated, careful speakers, vowels in unaccented syllables tend to become indistinct. Cultivated speakers whose pronunciation is normally standard often slur certain consonants and occasionally drop out entire syllables. We are all aware that, in speech, words often flow together without the pauses which, in writing, are shown by spaces. The "sound boundary" of a word or phrase—known to linguists as *juncture*—is nowhere indicated in any dictionary and is often blurred in speech.

Such speech habits are not necessarily faulty; so long as one's hearers understand without difficulty what is being said, no "error" occurs. In saying "boys and girls" or "bread and butter," for example, one can accent each word, but in formal and informal and standard and nonstandard speech, the phrases sound more like "boys'n girls" or "boysandgirls," "bread 'n butter" or "breadnbutter." In everyday speech, even educated and cultivated talkers may pronounce "It's all right" as "saw-right."

No one should be stiff and formal in making the sounds of speech, but we owe it to our hearers to speak clearly and acceptably. In the list that follows are words that nearly everyone occasionally mispronounces through haste or carelessness. Other words in the list cause trouble because of regional differences in speaking and in accenting words. Check your own speech habits for the pronunciations indicated. In informal talk, none of the mispronunciations can be called a downright error unless your hearer does not understand what you are saying. But make sure that informality and not ignorance is your guiding principle.

CARELESS PRONUNCIATION

accep (for *accept*)
accidently (for *accidentally*)
acrost (for *across*)
arncha (for *aren't you*)

asprin (for *aspirin*)
atakt (for *attack*)
athaletics (for *athletics*)
attackted (for *attacked*)

carmel (for *caramel*)
cartoon (for *carton*)
colyum (for *column*)
congradulate (for *congratulate*)
defnite (for *definite*)
dintcha (for *didn't you*)
disasterous (for *disastrous*)
distrik (for *district*)
doncha (for *don't you*)
drownded (for *drowned*)
envirament (for *environment*)
excep (for *except*)
famly (for *family*)
feller (for *fellow*)
finely (for *finally*)
gennelman (for *gentleman*)
gonna (for *going to*)
grievious (for *grievous*)
havncha (for *haven't you*)
hinderance (for *hindrance*)
histry (for *history*)
hundered (for *hundred*)
hyt-th (for *height*)
idenical (for *identical*)
incidently (for *incidentally*)
innerference (for *interference*)
inny (for *any*)
interduce (for *introduce*)
izda (for *is the*)
jester (for *gesture*)
jool (for *jewel*)
kep (for *kept*)
kintergarden (for *kindergarten*)
krool (for *cruel*)
laundery (for *laundry*)
literture (for *literature*)

mischievious (for *mischievous*)
modren (for *modern*)
monsterous (for *monstrous*)
nukular (for *nuclear*)
porpose (for *propose*)
practicly (for *practically*)
preform (for *perform*)
pressdent (for *president*)
probly (for *probably*)
progidy (for *prodigy*)
reaserch (for *research*)
reconize (for *recognize*)
rememberance (for *remembrance*)
represenative (for *representative*)
sawr (for *saw*)
shudder (for *shutter*)
similiar (for *similar*)
slep (for *slept*)
smothertam (for *some other time*)
suprise (for *surprise*)
strenth (for *strength*)
tempature (for *temperature*)
tempermental (for *temperamental*)
tenet (for *tenant*)
tradegy (for *tragedy*)
tremenjous (for *tremendous*)
umberella (for *umbrella*)
use to (for *used to*)
vallable (for *valuable*)
victry (for *victory*)
walkin (for *walking*)
wanna (for *want to*)
whachusay (for *what you say*)

whosit (for *who's it*)
willya (for *will you*)
wozzat (for *what's that*)
wunnerful (for *wonderful*)

wunst (for *once*)
youman (for *human*)
zat (for *that*)

Study this list of less than 100 often mispronounced words in ordinary use. If you are in doubt about the exact sounds and accents that are acceptable, consult your dictionary. If you are uncertain how you sound these words, ask a friend what he or she hears when you say them. This testing of yourself will give you a good idea of just how much a problem acceptable pronunciation is to you.

After you have mastered this list, give yourself a further test. Following is a list of 36 words (or expressions) that are repeatedly slurred, garbled, or misunderstood. If you don't use the mispronunciations shown or don't understand what the acceptable pronunciations are, consult your dictionary. Consult it anyway. In learning to speak more effectively there is no consultant more helpful or "ready, willing, and able."

accurate (not *akrit*)
ask (not *ast*)
bronchial (not *bronikal*)
cavalry (not *calvary*)
casual (not *casul*)
chic (not *shik*)
clique (not *click*)
chocolate (not *choclit*)
don't know (not *dunno*)
elite (not *ayelight*)
era (not *error*)
escape (not *ekskape*)
figure (not *figger*)
generally (not *genrally*)
genuine (not *genuwine*)
geography (not *geogafee*)
giant (not *jint*)
give me (not *gimme*)
hiccup (not *hikoff*)

Italian (not *eyetalian*)
manufacturer (not *manafacterer*)
metal (not *medal*)
particular (not *partikler*)
perspiration (not *prespiration*)
picture (not *pitcher*)
point (not *pernt*)
quay (not *kway*)
radio (not *raddio*)
real (not *ril*)
regular (not *reglar*)
something (not *sumpin*)
ticklish (not *tickalish*)
twice (not *twyst*)
veterinary (not *vetnary*)
what is it (not *whatsit*)
why don't you (not *whyncha*)

CHAPTER 5

What's Dialect All About?

"My dialect?" you ask. "Why, I don't have one. I talk just like the people around me."

Perhaps you do talk very much like the people with whom you associate. If so, that may be as it should be. An authority on the English language once suggested that we should "talk as our neighbors do, not better." But your answer to the question about dialect is partly incorrect. Also, if you do talk as others do, that may not be good enough to let you get ahead on your job.

Actually, you do have a dialect of some sort, no matter what your background is, how well you are educated, and how carefully you speak. Everyone—no exceptions—has his or her individual manner of speaking, a dialect exclusively his or her own and called an *idiolect*. (A dialect is a collection of idiolects, the speech patterns of a group of speakers.)

Another way to define dialect is to say that it is a variety of language distinguished from other varieties by such characteristics as grammar, word choice, and pronunciation. Dialect is not necessarily a form of "ridiculous" language or a set of "comical" speechways. The speech of one group is set off from that of another by geographical and social considerations. A Bostonian sounds like a Bostonian, not someone from the state of Georgia. An educated Bostonian does not sound like an uneducated Bostonian. An uneducated Georgian does not speak like an educated one. Several regionally accepted and therefore standard dialects are spoken in the United States. Within each regional dialect there are educated and uneducated varieties.

Look at the following examples of "educated" and "uneducated" speech. Each makes sense, but most hearers would feel that one variety is better—that is, more generally acceptable—than the other:

He does that every day.
He be doin' that every day.

Why isn't the room open yet?
How come the room ain't open yet?

It isn't always my fault.
It don't be always my fault.

Look at that woman with the thin legs.
Glim dat dame wid tin gams. (Looka dat gal wid da tin legs.)

He can walk as fast as I can.
He kin walk as fas'as I kin.

Although no single "correct" dialect exists, many people—possibly including your supervisors, fellow workers, and friends—find it difficult to accept the fact that your way of speaking can differ from theirs and still be standard—that is, acceptable or "correct." Before arguing with someone about a particular usage or pronunciation, it would help to find out if one way is as reputable and acceptable as another. But it is not easy to avoid the emotional attitudes about speech that lead to silly disputes.

Although no element of language can ever be considered entirely right or entirely wrong, each element should be looked at in terms of where and how it is used. Concerning every word and expression in the language it is sensible to ask (1) What social penalty, if any, attaches to it? (2) How frequent and how widespread is its use?

TESTS OF DIALECT

Any dialect in the United States is both proper and acceptable if it meets these tests:

1. It is characteristic of some major speech area in the United States, such as the North Atlantic states, the South, the Southwest, etc.
2. It is used by educated and cultured people, regardless of other considerations.

Apply these tests to the following examples of dialect. Each was written by a skilled author who was attempting to describe persons through the way they talked. Each tries to indicate the flavor of speech characteristic of a certain type of person in a certain area of the country. Each may sound strange to your ear because each fails one or both of the tests indicated.

1. A passage from William Faulkner's *Sanctuary*, a novel dealing with the lives of largely uneducated blacks and whites in Mississippi:

   . . . Beside the entrance a crude ladder mounted. "Better wait twell I git up," the man said. "Hit's putty rotten; mought not hold us both."

   "Why don't you fix it, then? Don't you use it every day?"

   "Hit's helt all right, so fur," the other said. He mounted. Then Gowan followed, through the trap, into yellow-barred gloom where the level sun fell through the broken walls and roof. "Walk where I do," the man said. "You'll tromp on a loose boa'd and find yoself downstairs befo you know hit." He picked his way across the floor and dug an earthenware jug from a pile of rotting hay in the corner. "One place he won't look fer hit," he said. "Skeered of sp'ilin them gal's hands of hisn."

2. Remarks by an uneducated barber in Michigan, from a short story by Ring Lardner entitled "Haircut":

   You can see for yourself that this ain't no New York City and besides that, the most of the boys works all day and don't have no leisure to drop in here and get themselves prettied up.

   She'd came on about the same business I had. Her mother had been doctorin for years with Doc Gamble and Doc Foote and without no results. So she'd heard they was a new doc in town and decided to give him a try.

Meanwile everybody in town was wise to Julie's being wild mad over the Doc. I don't suppose she had any idear how her face changed when him and her was together; of course she couldn't of, or she'd of kep away from him.

3. Speech in rural New England as recorded by Eugene O'Neill in his play, *Desire Under the Elms*:

"Whar in tarnation d'ye s'pose he went?"

"Dunno. He druv off in the buggy, all spick an' span, with the mare all breshed an' shiny, druv off clackin' his tongue an' wavin' his whip. I remember it right well. . . . I yells 'whar ye goin', Paw?' an' he hauls up by the stone wall a jiffy. His old snake eyes was glitterin' in the sun."

4. Remarks of a Nevada rancher in *The Ox-Bow Incident* by Walter Van Tilburg Clark:

"I hate the stink of an Injun, but an Injun smells sweet comparin' to a railroad man. If we'd wanted to keep this country for decent people, we'da helped the Injuns bust up the railroad, yes, by God, we woulda. And that's the same law you're tryin' to hold us up for, ain't it—the kind of law that'll give a murderer plenty of time to get away and cover up, and then help him find his excuses by the book. You and your posses are waitin'. I say get goin' before we're cooled off, and the lily liver that's in half these new dudes gets time to pisen' em again, so we gotta just set back and listen to Judge Tyler spout his law and order crap."

5. A passage from John Steinbeck's novel, *The Grapes of Wrath*:

"I knowed you wasn't Oklahomy folks. You talk queer, kinda—that ain't no blame, you understan."

"Ever'body says words different," said Ivy. "Arkansas folks says'em different, and Oklahomy folks says'em different. And we seen a lady from Massachusetts, an' she said'em differentest of all. Couldn' hardly make out what she was sayin'.''

6. A paragraph from a newspaper column by Leonard Lyons: At a supper party in London, actor John Loder was seated next to an attractive French woman who lives in Italy. Loder, who knows the country well, asked in what part she lived. She replied, "In ze Norz." "What beautiful lakes you have," he said. "How can you see zem?" she asked. "Zey are under ze table."

The most publicized dialect of a small regional area in this country is that of Brooklyn, a part of New York City. Cartoonists, comedians, columnists, and movies have made much of such examples of Brooklynese as these:

dese for *these* and *dose* for *those*
dem for *them*, and *da* for *the* (*dem* were *da* good days)
bunking for *bumping* (*bunking* into people on the street)

toidy-toid for *thirty-third*	*pernts* for *points*
udder for *other*	*berled* for *boiled*
goils for *girls*	*erl* for *oil*
moidered for *murdered*	*Noo Joisey* for *New Jersey*
boid for *bird*	*boig* for *burg*

Brooklynese fails both of the tests mentioned. That is, Brooklyn does not represent a major speech area. Also, despite the fact that Brooklynese is fully acceptable in certain limited circles, hundreds of thousands of educated and cultured Brooklynites don't talk this way at all.

REGIONAL DIALECTS IN THE U.S.

Brooklynese is only one of many small "pockets of dialect spoken throughout the United States. Each of these narrowly local dialects is acceptable within its own area because it is used by many people living there and is nearly always understood.

But much narrowly dialectal usage should be avoided because it wouldn't be understood on a national basis.

Would everyone understand this notice tacked onto a door in Pennsylvania Dutch country: "Button don't bell. Bump.''? To those who can translate the message as "Please knock because the bell is out of order," the expression is vivid. To others, the sign would be meaningless.

Equally meaningless would be this sign posted in a North Carolina country store: KWITTIN CREDIT TILL I GET MY OUTINS IN. The sign seems quaint when it is translated to mean "I shall extend no further credit to anyone who has not made full payment for goods already received."

The Western, Southwestern, Southern, and Northeastern areas of the United States are rich in local dialects that add flavor to speech but that may be misunderstood. For a person living in one of those areas, such expressions are hard to detect, because as a speaker or listener he accepts them as reputable and casually assumes that they are universally understood since he himself has heard and used them from childhood. Words and combinations of words used locally are labeled by dictionaries according to the geographical area where they are most common.

Because dialect involves usage and vocabulary as well as pronunciation, it may be difficult always to remember that expressions familiar to you may not make complete sense to all who hear you. If you wish every listener from another section of the country (or from some other English-speaking country) to understand you, avoid using such expressions as these:

Western: *coulee* (narrow valley); *dogie, dogy* (motherless calf); *mesquite* (spiny shrub).

Southwestern: *mesa* (rocky hill); *longhorn* (formerly a kind of cattle).

Southern: *butternuts* (brown overalls); *lightwood* (pitchy pine); *hoecake* (cake of Indian meal); *corn pone* (corn bread); *turn* (armful); *snap beans* (string beans).

Northeastern: *selectman* (town official); *moosewood* (striped maple); *down-Easter* (native New Englander, especially one from Maine); *skunk cabbage* (skunkweed); *johnny cake* (corn meal cake).

Try to keep in mind that the talk of millions of Americans, regardless of what section of the country they live in, is flavored with the sounds, accents, and vocabulary of many languages. Depending upon where you live and what your background is, your speech has been influenced by one or the other of such languages as Italian, German, Spanish, French, Polish, Yiddish, Greek, Hungarian, Norwegian, and Dutch. The talk of some blacks and of others closely associated with blacks contains traces of African dialects. A considerable part of Brooklynese is derived from such languages as German, Yiddish, and Gaelic. Reflecting geographical origins are the speech sounds of many Mexican-Americans, Puerto Ricans, Cubans, and American Indians.

In short, the heritage of many different races and nationalities has helped to make the United States the great country it is. If your way of speaking is colored by traces of other languages, you have no cause to be ashamed. Instead, you may rightly regard your way of speaking as a kind of distinction, a mark of identity to be proud of. Thousands of American men and women who came from what some might consider "disadvantaged" backgrounds have risen to great prominence without ever forsaking the way they talked in their formative years.

Actually, some foreign accents and word choices that result in speech strange to your ears and mine are often considered not only acceptable but attractive. Large numbers of actors, actresses, government officials, motion picture producers, and other leading executives have not been held back by their dialects. Office workers, especially secretaries, who have a British accent are sometimes considered superior by some business firms. Advertisers on television and radio often use persons with a Swedish accent to sell grooming aids and tobacco. Persons with German accents are considered effective salesmen for beer; those with Italian accents are employed to sell wines, salad dressings, and condiments.

YOUR DIALECT MAY WORK AGAINST YOU

Despite these reasons for not being guilty about a part of your heritage, you may feel that your particular dialect is not an asset but a liability. If so, you may wish to work on any part of your dialect that seems to be holding you back. In doing so, however, always keep in mind that although you may consider your accent to be damaging, it is wise to pay attention to what you have to say, the words you choose, your idiomatic usage, and the rhythm of your speech. These matters are a much more important part of dialect than is accent alone.

If your speech clearly shows that your native tongue is not English and if you feel that how you talk may be damaging to your progress, you may wish to work on it just as the author had to work when he lived in France and had to spend much time in trying to learn to speak French without offending French men and women. It takes a long time—perhaps years for most people—to rid oneself of a foreign accent. But you may feel that the effort is worthwhile. If you so feel, then it is.

In trying to rid yourself of a foreign accent, consider these recommendations:

1. Talk slowly, more slowly in English than you speak in your native tongue.
2. Listen carefully and closely to persons who speak "good" English.
3. Speak English as often as you can. This suggestion is especially important if some other language is normally spoken in your home.
4. Speaking softly and slurring words will highlight your foreign accent, not hide it.
5. Always keep in mind that English is a stress language. Practice such accented syllables as DOLL.ar and com.-MER.cial.
6. Try to form the habit of ending sentences (statements) with a falling inflection.
7. Use a rising inflection only to connect ideas and at the ends of questions.

8. Practice linking (joining) words. Words should be said clearly, but the pattern of English speech runs words together in a smooth flow.
9. As often as possible, read aloud to yourself a newspaper or magazine. Try to listen to your voice as you read.
10. As time permits, listen carefully to the radio, television, talking records, and tapes.

Losing a foreign accent is not a simple task. Even more difficult is trying to perfect the rhythms and idiomatic usage of a language that is not native to you. But you can console yourself by realizing that thousands of English-speaking men and women are facing similar barriers while working in foreign countries. For them and perhaps for you, differences in usage and language structure are handicapping to a speaker who is expected to perform in a system that demands the use of standard structure, style, and usage.

Speaking in any one of several acceptable dialects is important in almost any kind of work. If the dialect you have is not generally acceptable, you must face the fact that it has resulted from your cultural background, your nationality, or your geographical origin. These matters have been fixed for all time.

However, the improvement of one's accustomed manner of speaking is not impossible and not difficult if it is worked at steadily and carefully. In addition, keep in mind that dialect can be better understood, wrestled with, and improved by attention to word choice, idiom, and the rhythm of your speech than by too great concern over pronunciation and accent. These other approaches are treated in separate chapters in this book. Work on the problems you have with an unacceptable dialect but don't make the mistake of thinking that pronunciation is everything that counts. It isn't.

One final word: no one can speak so carefully, faultlessly, and clearly that everyone will accept and approve of his every statement. But each of us can learn to speak in ways that are generally acceptable and that are *understood*. Communication is the "without which nothing" of all speech. Each of us can say the prayer uttered by the poet Geoffrey Chaucer some 600 years ago:

> And since there is so great diversity
> In English and the writing of our speech,
> For lack of language may you never be
> Miswritten or mismetered, I beseech.
> And read or sung, wherever your words may reach
> May you be understood, to God I pray.

CHAPTER 6

How Do You Sound?

Your voice is as unique as your footprints and fingerprints. The sounds you make differ from those made by everyone else in the entire world. Your voice can be picked out in the dark. It can be recognized over the telephone at a distance of thousands of miles. And the person who hears you in the dark or over the telephone may not only recognize you but be able to tell something about what you are really thinking and how you feel.

People catalog us in their minds through our voices. Entire industries are voice-conscious: radio and television announcers and broadcasters; telephone operators; actors and actresses; airline pilots, flight attendants, and passenger service personnel; train and bus announcers; preachers; politicians; and trial lawyers.

No surer index of personality exists than the human voice. A few minutes conversation will reveal to an observant stranger an astonishing amount of information about one's background, line of work, and personality. Oliver Wendell Holmes, himself an accomplished talker, once remarked: "All of a man's antecedents and possibilities are summed up in a single utterance, which gives at once the gauge of his education and his mental organization." Holmes' statement may be an exaggeration. But you and I know that we are constantly sizing up by their voices people with whom we come in contact. Voices do attract or repel us.

Consider these comments made by personnel managers interviewed while this book was being written: "Anyone with a

harsh, rough voice doesn't belong anywhere in our business."
"Some employees have such uncertain, wavering voices that
their fellow workers don't pay them much attention." "A person
with a thin, weak voice will have a tough time being considered
for an executive spot." "The main reason some people stay
stuck in the same jobs is that when they don't sound sullen and
mad, they sound sarcastic and tactless." "People are constantly
coming into this office asking for work that will let them contact
more people, but most of them can't be moved because they
sound argumentative and buttheaded or modest and shy."

No one is born with a speaking voice. Everyone is born with
speaking equipment, a mechanism for voice. How we sound is
the result of many considerations and conditions, either self-
made or brought about by circumstances into which we have
fallen. The voice you have depends upon

1. The vocal habits formed during infancy, childhood, and
   adolescence.
2. The influence of members of your family, associates, and
   friends.
3. The kinds of work you have done and are doing.
4. Your personality and temperament.
5. The education you have had, in and out of school.
6. The physical make-up of your voice mechanism (nasal
   passages, the size and shape of your mouth, your teeth,
   your vocal bands).
7. General health (muscles, physical tone, breathing apparatus).

LISTEN TO YOUR OWN VOICE

No matter how "good" or "bad" your voice is, you can improve it if you know what to do and will make an effort. The
first requirement is finding out how you sound. You've heard
your voice thousands of times, but have you ever listened to
it?

Walk to the corner of a quiet room, face it, and cup your

ears. Say a few words in your normal voice. That strange sound you may never really have heard before is *you*. Does your voice sound confident, sociable, cheerful, sincere, alert, enthusiastic— or none of these? Does it sound nervous, hesitant, weak, thin, boastful, angry—or none of these?

If you are not satisfied with your answers to these questions, put them to a friend or acquaintance. What qualities does he or she think your voice possesses? Then go a step further. Ask yourself the following questions and try to answer them honestly:

1. Do I articulate well (speak clearly in distinct syllables)?
2. Do I speak with proper (enough, not too much) volume?
3. Do I have enough power (strength, firmness of tone)?
4. Is my voice pleasant?
5. Is my voice expressive?
6. Is my voice alive?

If you are still not certain about the quality of your voice, do one or both of two things: (1) ask for an objective opinion from someone else or (2) make a recording of your voice and play it back. If you are really honest with yourself, it should be easy to decide whether your voice is nasal, monotonous, graveled, strident, slurred, whining, tired, or hesitant. If you determine that it is any of these, keep squarely in mind that it will make an unfortunate impression on others and will help to hold you back from the advancement you wish.

In studying your voice, ask not only how it *sounds* but how it *looks* and *feels*. A good speaking voice sounds easy on the ears, firmly based, and alive. It *feels* relaxed, open, and effortless. It *looks* how? Well, talk while facing a mirror. Is your jaw relaxed? Are your facial muscles free from strain and tension? Is your mouth pulled back at the corners? Does your tongue incorrectly peep through your lips? Are your shoulders at rest, your chest not heaving, your throat not tense? If it's hard for you to decide how your own voice sounds, looks, and feels, try observing how other people talk. If you look carefully and listen attentively, you can make observations which you can then apply to your own voice.

If, after careful study of your voice, you are not satisfied with it, give first attention to the way you breathe. The basis of all tone production is breathing. Air taken into your lungs is let out through action of chest muscles and the diaphragm, another name for the midriff—a wall of tendons and muscles between the cavities of chest and abdomen. Expelled air passes between your vocal cords in a vibrating manner that produces tone. Put another way, the "motor" of your voice is an exhaled breath stream. If your motor is not working properly, your voice will suffer.

Practice breathing deeply enough and often enough to maintain a suitable, steady stream of air. When you are speaking, try to inhale deeply, taking air into what seems the bottom of your lungs. When you exhale, your diaphragm will push air toward your windpipe and larnyx, vocal bands that can be called "vibrators."

Next, keep your mouth open and your throat muscles relaxed so that sounds started by the vocal cords can be built up in the mouth and head cavities and come freely from your mouth. Your throat, nose, and mouth are called "resonators," or "amplifiers," but they cannot work properly unless they have an adequate amount of air to start with.

It's especially important to make a real effort to relax your throat muscles. This is essential when you feel tense, hurried, and nervous. Haven't you ever noticed how strained the throat of a worried person looks when he or she talks to you? Relaxed throat muscles help to send tones forward out of the mouth without fluttering and fading.

Now comes the problem of articulation, the process of modifying breath or voice with your tongue, lips, gums, teeth, and soft and hard palates. These articulators are the agents that help you to speak with the least muscular effort and assist with the clarity and distinctness of sounds produced. You have a right to expect your voice to operate with minimum effort and maximum effectiveness—exactly as you want your car, refrigerator, or dishwasher to perform. A trained voice works this way. If your voice is untrained, or badly trained, regular practice with breathing and muscle-relaxing will improve it immensely.

In every speaking situation, regardless of whether you are talking to one person, a small group, or a large audience, your voice should be (1) audible, (2) animated, and (3) well-pitched.

No one wishes to strain his ears. No one likes to talk with a person who mumbles, swallows words, or turns away his or her head. You can and should adapt the volume of your voice to the size of any group listening and to any competing sound that is present. Soft voices are pleasant, but only when they are audible. Powerful voices can be effective, but only when they are not loud and strident.

No matter to whom you are talking, your voice should be lively and animated. Animation comes from the vigor with which you speak, the energy you put into your voice and body. Being animated need not involve gestures, grimaces, bodily contortions, or loudness. It certainly does not involve droning away in listless, spiritless, languid, and indifferent tones.

Pitch has to do with the loudness or highness of sound. Every voice has a normal key, a base line from which it moves up or down in steps or glides. If your voice is high-pitched (and more people's voices are than not), try to lower it. In doing this, don't try to reach and stay on a base that is uncomfortable and that causes muscular tension. An effective, pleasant voice covers a range in pitch. A monotonous voice stays largely on one pitch level. Don't you get bored listening to someone who never varies the pitch of his or her voice? Aren't you more likely to pay attention to someone with a flexible voice?

Yes, with thought, care, and attention you can improve your voice, no matter how it sounds, looks, and feels. The only persons who can't have some physical problem requiring the attention of a surgeon or orthodontist. If you have tried to improve your voice through suggestions offered in this chapter and are not satisfied with results, then get from your local library any of a number of helpful books on voice training and voice control. If you wish, you can visit a speech consultant professionally. A capable, reliable teacher can readily help you in improving the pitch, flexibility, and volume of your voice.

Whatever you do, don't neglect the role your voice plays in getting, holding, and advancing in a job. One's voice is not so important as character, ability, industry, and reliability, but it deserves more attention than you have probably ever given it.

Speech finely framed delighteth the ears.
The Apocrypha

CHAPTER 7

The Art of Conversation

The first six chapters of this book discuss pronunciation, dialect, and voice. They deal with *how* we say words more than with *what* we say: the choice and use of words to express in sentences what we think and feel. Before tackling the varied problems of vocabulary, let's consider three everyday situations in which nearly everyone is constantly involved: *conversation, use of the telephone*, and *listening*.

Each of these activities has a direct influence upon the job security and job improvement of everyone engaged in business or a profession of any kind. Each involves talking, but none more directly than what might be called the "art" or "business" or "practice" of conversation.

How many times during each working day do you talk with or to someone else? If you are like most of us, you can't count them. And yet you realize that hardly any day goes by without dozens, scores, or even hundreds of occasions on which you exchange a few words or a great many with other people. Many of these exchanges probably are brief and apparently unimportant. But it is possible that every remark you make to someone else has a bearing, direct or indirect, upon how that person feels about and reacts to you.

On some occasions you will say something to a person who is in a position to fire you, raise your salary, or recommend you for a better job. (A personnel manager interviewed while this book was being prepared insisted that the maintenance supervisor of the building where he works was promoted from his job as an elevator operator largely because of the friendly, cordial way in which he spoke to all who rode with him.) How and whether you say "Good morning" or "Good night" to others where you work may be more important than you realize. Even more significant are longer conversational exchanges that tell much about you, your attitudes, and your personality.

If it isn't conversation, what is it that attracts you to certain persons and causes you to avoid others? (Let's leave money, love, and lust out of this discussion.) Why is some individual usually the center of attention during a coffee break or at lunch time? In any place you've ever worked, hasn't someone always seemed more popular, more sought after, than all others? More often than not, isn't the person who "gets ahead" a good and interesting talker, a capable conversationalist?

Away from work, you like to be with certain people and try to stay away from others. Many considerations are involved in making a date, deciding with whom to spend a leisure hour, or debating which invitation to accept for a party. Don't overlook the fact that your choice may be based at least partly on how much you like or dislike the conversation of others involved. The novelist Somerset Maugham once asked "Do you know that conversation is one of the greatest pleasures of life?" If your conversation gives pleasure to others—or at least does not offend them—you have a far better chance to get ahead with whatever it is you have in mind.

If you can improve your conversations with people at work and at home, you will achieve these worthwhile results:

1. You will have an increased ability to make friends.
2. You will be helped in taking a place of leadership in your home, your club, and your community.
3. You will increase your chances of getting ahead in whatever kind of work you do.
4. You will add to your self-esteem and self-respect and expand your capacity for self-expression.

Conversation is the most universal of all kinds of social activity, as well as the most important way of communicating with others. A good conversationalist, one who has something interesting to say and who listens courteously and attentively, is welcome anywhere at any time. Lack of opportunity for exchange of talk with others can produce irritation, boredom, and even serious mental disorders. One of man's fundamental needs is to express himself to others. One of the most severe of all prison punishments is solitary confinement.

If people are more frustrated today than ever before, if conversation is indeed a lost art, perhaps two reasons are that people feel too hurried to talk *with* others and too often are engaged in watching TV or listening to the radio. True conversation is a two-way street that cannot be passed through hurriedly and thoughtlessly, at work or at play.

A good and rewarding conversation—a genuine meeting of minds—has little or nothing to do with talkativeness. Chatter about such a subject as the weather, clothes, and food is rarely good conversation, no matter how cleverly words may fly. Conversation, no matter how brief, becomes worthwhile, a stimulating pastime, when it represents an open, honest, thoughtful exchange of facts and opinions dealing with more than just superficial subjects. Glibness may save you the trouble of making clear your position in a conversation, but it wastes the time of both speaker and listener.

Conversing with others comes naturally to some people, regardless of their education, knowledge, or position. Such persons seem to like others, to be interested in them as people, and to be willing to listen to their points of view. These attitudes and abilities of born conversationalists provide clues for anyone wishing to become a better *talker with* (not *to*) others. Here are a few suggestions.

IMPROVING THE WAY YOU TALK WITH OTHERS

1. Many a person has acquired a reputation as an excellent conversationalist primarily because he is a good listener. Even the most unsure and unskilled speaker can be, or appear to be, truly interested in a partner and in what he or she is saying. In fact, the expression on one's face may show interest and antici-

pation (or the reverse) even before a conversation begins. As a good conversationalist, you may or may not agree with what is being said, but you should not gaze away from your partner. Try to show by attention and brief comments or questions that you are reacting in some way to what you are hearing. Additional comment on listening appears in another chapter.

2. Try to be straightforward and sincere but also courteous, tactful, and friendly. A spirited discussion may be heated—a group of people will seldom wholly agree about any topic of real importance—but one can state an opinion frankly and firmly without being rude and without hurting others. Your partner's feelings can be as easily wounded as yours. If he starts a joke you have already heard, you can listen quietly or can tactfully sidetrack him; you don't have to say, "That's an old one. It stinks." If your partner makes a misstatement, you can courteously point this out when she finishes her statement; you don't have to interrupt with "Can't you ever get your facts straight?" or "You've got it all wrong" or "That's a lie" or "Only a fool believes that." The most exciting conversations are those in which people express opposing points of view, but talk can be even-tempered even when it is argumentative.

3. The best conversations are give-and-take affairs. Being a good listener is fundamental, but one should also have something to say oneself. An effective conversation resembles a game of tennis in that action shifts from person to person. Two persons cannot play the game of either tennis or conversation if one holds the ball continuously. Be careful to do some attentive listening *and* some thoughtful talking in every conversation. When one person does all the talking, what follows is a *monologue*. A genuine conversation is a *dialogue*, an exchange between two or more persons.

4. If your conversational partner is not an intimate friend or member of your family, try to find out as much as you tactfully can about him or her. For example, if you are left with a stranger at a party, the guest of honor at a reception, or a visitor to your office, try drawing that person out rather than talking about yourself. You may learn some interesting facts. Even if you don't, your companion will be flattered by your interest

(even if it is partly assumed) and will remember you as a superb conversationalist.

5. Try to keep informed about subjects of timely interest: political affairs, current events, personalities in the news, fashion trends, sports, art, music, and literature. Read as much as you can: a daily newspaper, books, worthwhile magazines. Try to remember good stories you hear or read, amusing or interesting incidents that happen to you or your friends, funny or significant events you see or read about. People who assume a know-it-all attitude make poor conversationalists, but so do emptyheaded ones who can talk about only what they had for dinner.

6. Study every conversation you have an opportunity to hear or engage in. Analysis of conversations will indicate that the best talkers are those with the largest fund of interesting experiences and observations, or, better yet, the greatest familiarity with subjects of most interest to people in the circle. You will also notice that the most capable conversationalists do not talk constantly but are capable of keeping quiet.

7. Practice conversation. Join in good talk whenever you can. Listen in on conversations when you have an opportunity to do so without being a pest or an eavesdropper. After listening to a conversation on TV or radio, practice to yourself or with a friend your own responses to questions rasied or topics developed.

8. Even in informal conversations, try to speak as clearly and as effectively as you can. We owe it to our conversational partners to be as alert, as informed, and as communicative as we possibly can. Avoiding mistakes in choosing, using, and pronouncing words is far more than a negative effort toward effective conversation.

Don't slight these eight remarks and suggestions. Pay attention to them so that you will be paid dividends in every part of your social and working life. Your office manager, section boss, supervisor, or foreman will react favorably if you show some interest in the problems he or she has. Try to avoid sweeping statements if there is any way to be specific. Cultivate the habit of disagreeing agreeably. When you can, take the cotton from your ears and put it in your mouth. That is, listen more and talk less, especially when you are conversing with someone in authority. *Above all, when you are talking, get to the point, make it, and shut up.* Boring details will kill interest in any conversation, whether at home, in the street, or at work.

Also, give *added* thought to the way you talk with others. Honest answers to the following questions may indicate why you are getting ahead or falling behind with acquaintances, friends, and business associates:

1. Do I contradict others without good reason?
2. Do I interrupt someone who is talking?
3. Am I too frank and blunt in what I say?
4. Do I sound sarcastic and nasty?
5. Have I a "chip on my shoulder"?
6. Is my favorite topic of conversation myself?
7. Am I quick to hand out unasked-for advice?
8. Does it bore me to listen to someone else?
9. Do I "talk down" to others, making them feel inferior?
10. Are my remarks so flat and final that they shut the door on further talk?

Conversation is self-expression, all right, providing us with chances to let off steam. It's a safety valve by means of which we boast about ourselves and "get even" with others and the entire world. Being human, most of us will continue to use conversation for these purposes. And yet conversation will result in direct benefits when we learn to look upon it as a sharing of interests, a pooling of information, and a bringing together of people and ideas.

One of the wisest comments ever made about conversation (and indeed all forms of communication) is this remark of Henry David Thoreau's: "It takes two to speak truth—one to speak and another to hear."

CHAPTER 8

Courtesy Over the Wires

In talking your way to a better job, never forget that much of your talk is done over the telephone.

A telephone instrument is impersonal. Also, in a telephone conversation you do not see the person with whom you are conversing. Therefore, you may forget how much added pressure is put upon your voice and manner of speaking. Telephone talk has as many requirements as face-to-face conversation, some of them different but all of them important.

Your telephone manners are not likely to get you fired or promoted, but how you handle the telephone has at least some bearing upon which of these happens to you.

Many places of business provide employees with specific instructions about making and answering calls and giving out company or product information. If you have such a set of directions, follow it carefully and exactly. Your superiors will notice whether or not you do and may react to you and your job performance accordingly.

15 TIPS ON TELEPHONE USE

The suggestions that follow should be ignored if they are not in line with prescribed telephone policies where you work. But if there is no conflict or if you do not have directions, consider the following remarks:

1. Over the telephone, use the same tone of voice you would in direct conversation. Since whomever you are talking to can't

see you, your voice is your only contact and thus takes on added significance. It can give your listener the impression that you are surly or helpful, unconcerned or interested, nasty or pleasant.

2. The telephone is not a high fidelity instrument. Although most telephone service is remarkably efficient in transmitting sounds, it's important to speak even more clearly and distinctly than you would in direct conversation. Don't slur and don't mumble. Try to make your voice sound alive and energetic, not emotionless. Open your mouth. Don't talk with a pencil, pen, food, a cigarette, a pipe, or a paper clip in it.

3. Speak at what is your normal speed, provided that rate is slow enough to be readily understood. As you know, more people talk rapidly than slowly. They forget that the ear is slower than the tongue. Of course, dragging, lazy speech is also a problem, but a much rarer one than rapidfire delivery.

4. Speak directly into the mouthpiece with your lips not more than one inch away and not less than 1/2 inch. If you are calling from a noisy place, cup one hand around the mouthpiece as an aid to your hearer.

5. Many telephone users like to "visit" over the wires, but all calls—and especially business ones—should be to the point. If you are talking with a friend, save the chatter and gossip for lunch time or after hours. If you are talking to a busy person, close friend or not, say what needs to be said, hear what needs to be heard, and hang up.

6. When your telephone rings, answer it as quickly as possible. You don't have to drop anything and everything instantly, but it is courteous, thoughtful, and time-saving to keep your caller waiting no longer than necessary.

7. When making a call, give your name (or position) to the person answering. (If your place of work prescribes a formula for this practice, follow it carefully.) The game of "guess who" is juvenile and has no place in the business world, or indeed anywhere. Of course if you are calling a friend or close acquaintance who instantly recognizes your voice, you can be guided accordingly. Yet you normally have as much obligation to say who you are when making a call as if you had knocked

on a stranger's door, called at his or her home, or walked into a strange office.

8. Follow the procedures recommended by your place of business for answering the phone with "hello" or your name, position, or division. Normally, it is time-saving to answer with your name when you are at work. At home and in all entirely social situations, the person answering has a right to know who is "invading privacy" before revealing his or her identity.

9. Have a sheet of paper (pad, notebook) and pencil or pen at hand when answering the phone. It is discourteous and annoying to a caller to have to wait while you scrounge around for something on which to write a message or number. If you have to "hold the line" momentarily, don't annoy your telephone partner and hurt his ear by slamming down your receiver on a hard surface. Don't bang down the phone at the end of a conversation, either; the person at the other end may still be connected.

10. Many companies request or require even "top" personnel to answer their own phones whenever possible. This practice often pays dividends because callers get the impression that the company being called is courteous, efficient, interested, and means business. Also, no matter how important you are in a company, don't have someone place a call for you and then keep the person called waiting until you are free or disposed to talk. Gamesmanship has no real place in telephone talk.

11. If you know the work routine and schedule of busy persons, try to time your calls to them to suit their convenience. Calls made during the first and last half hours of a business day are often not so productive as those made at other times. Timing your call is especially important if the planned conversation is necessarily going to take considerable time.

12. Most businesses frown on personal calls. Occasionally, an emergency does come up. And yet many people have been held back or dismissed because they insisted on using cost-free business phones for personal calls. As much as you can, discourage friends from taking up your employer's paid-for time with idle calls to you.

13. When calling a number, wait long enough—say four or

five or more rings—for an answer. You know yourself how annoying it is to reach your phone just as someone hangs up.

14. Courtesy over the telephone is never out of place. "May I ask who's calling, please" should never be necessary, but if it is, it sounds better than "Who's this?" or "What's your name?" or "Whaddaya want?" When you make a call and an unfamiliar voice answers, it's more courteous to ask "Is this Extension 605?" or "Is this 765-7582?" than to demand "What's your number?" Better to say "Hold the line, please" than "Hang on" or "Hold it a minute" or "Wait up." When you do resume an interrupted call, your hearer will appreciate your saying "Thank you for waiting."

15. Try never to lose your temper over the telephone. Admittedly, certain calls are annoying, upsetting, and even stupid. A misunderstanding in face-to-face talk, however, can sometimes be cleared up by further conversation. It's easy to slam down the phone angrily and block all chances for peacemaking and understanding.

If you feel that your telephone manners and methods need further attention, ask the advice of someone who seems to you to handle phone situations well. Such a person may be your foreman or supervisor or office manager or a fellow employee. In addition, you can telephone the business representative of your local telephone company. He or she will see that you get a copy of a booklet on telephone use, such as many companies have available.

Telephone talk is a very real extension of yourself. Always try to remember that you can do your place of work good or harm by your use of the phone. Even more to the point is that you directly affect your own job in the same way.

Good nature is more agreeable in conversation than wit and gives a certain air to the countenance which is more amiable than beauty.
Joseph Addison

CHAPTER 9

What Are Ears For?

That poor listeners are expensive and expendable employees is increasingly recognized in the business world. Supervisors, office managers, foremen, and other executive persons send up a steady stream of complaints about people who "don't listen," who "don't get it right," who "make mistakes" because they don't hear and do what they're told. True, directions, orders, and suggestions are often not given clearly, but a good listener will recognize this and ask questions until what he or she is told *is* made clear.

No one can estimate how many people have been fired because they made mistakes due to faulty listening. It's impossible to calculate how much money has been lost because of unheard or partly heard directions and requests. And what is true of the world of business is equally true of life outside office and factory.

Many of our most important affairs depend on listening. What does a jury do? It listens—sometimes to millions of words of testimony—and then makes up its mind about the case on trial. The way one votes in an election depends in part upon ability (or inability) to listen. Listening situations and opportunities face each of us many times every day. What else can and should one expect in a nation that has tens of millions of television sets; more radios than television sets, and several million *new* telephone installations every year?

What has all this to do with learning to "say it right," with "getting ahead" at work? Simply this: profiting from listening opportunities and situations can rapidly increase one's own ability to talk.

For example, compared to reading, listening is often a faster and more efficient way to gather information. If you need to learn something about a subject quickly, you can usually find an authority who will talk to you in terms you can understand. Further, if you don't understand something he or she says, you can ask a question and get immediate clarification, thus entering into the conversation and gaining added experience in both listening and speaking.

Again, writing, including manuals and work schedules, that seems difficult can often be better understood when spoken aloud. Much great literature—the plays of Shakespeare, for example—were written only to be heard. Reading aloud and listening to yourself will increase your ability to shape and pronounce words and to improve the quality of your speaking voice. Nearly everyone can find a friend to join in reading aloud.

Good listening is one of the best of all ways for improving your speaking ability. This fact probably stems from childhood, when we learned to talk by listening to and imitating our elders. The principle remains, regardless of how old we are or how accomplished as speakers. We can and should learn to speak better by listening to speakers of all sorts in face-to-face conversations, over the telephone, on television and radio, and in movies.

Unfortunately, most people have acquired harmful listening habits that defeat efforts in learning to listen while listening to learn. Honestly consider the following faulty listening habits. Do you recognize any of them in yourself? If you do, by trying to replace a bad habit with a good one you can improve your ability to listen and speak more effectively.

1. *Quick dismissal of a subject as dull and uninteresting.*

If a speaker's material seems boring, some of us use that impression as a reason for not listening. We assume that if a person's words are not stimulating, he must have nothing to say that is worth hearing. Before we "tune out" we should recall that there are no uninteresting subjects, only uninterested persons. When one forms the habit of listening attentively, many previously dull subjects take on new life. Have you never become friends with, or even fallen in love with, someone you once considered dull and uninteresting? Also, if a speaker and his material *are* unappealing, analyzing the reasons for this condition can help you to avoid them when you are doing the talking.

2. *Supersensitive listening.*

Some of us find it difficult to listen to anything that does not agree with our own thoughts. Hearing statements that we do not like, we start planning an answer and stop listening to what the speaker is saying. It's better to hear the speaker out and to make final judgments after he or she has finished. One is not listening when planning a counterattack; one is not engaging in conversation when he has "tuned out" the speaker and "tuned in" his personal train of thought.

3. *Avoiding difficult explanations.*

Many listeners give up quickly when something is difficult to understand. They blame the speaker for not making his points clearer and simpler. The remedy: go out of your way to hear those speaking on topics that are hard to grasp and stick with the subject from beginning to end. Listening requires practice. In addition, it is possible that the experience of listening to difficult material will provide ideas and suggest methods for making your own talk more interesting and understandable.

4. *Finding fault with a speaker's appearance or delivery.*

Sometimes we do not pay attention to what a speaker is saying because we become involved in the way he talks and looks. If his manner of speaking or the way he looks creates an unfavorable impression, we lose interest. Or a speaker's looks or manner may cause romantic or other images that are equally distracting. The most important task in listening is to learn what the speaker says, not how he or she looks when saying it. Nevertheless, for our own benefit, we should notice carefully the mannerisms of speech and behavior that add to or detract from the effectiveness of what is being said. Trying to avoid or to imitate such characteristics will help to improve our own speaking ability.

3 IMPORTANT STEPS IN LISTENING

Three important steps are involved in listening of any kind: (1) hearing, (2) understanding, and (3) responding.

First, actually hearing what is being said requires attention and concentration. One or more of the four faults mentioned in preceding paragraphs may cause the inattention. Actually, however, many of us have never formed the habit of paying attention for more than a few seconds at a time. When someone starts talking to us, we listen at first but then close our ears or start thinking about matters unconnected with what we should be hearing. Really hearing and keeping on hearing takes effort and practice.

Have you ever been surprised at how much more some people can remember of a talk, a lecture, a meeting, or a set of oral directions than you can? Have you ever wondered at the ability of a newspaper reporter or trial lawyer to recall details of a long speech or extended conversation? Their success comes from close attention. It's not a matter of memory alone. We have to "get" something before we can "forget" it. Start really trying to hear what you are told by a supervisor, manager, or fellow-worker. The effort will pay off, sooner or later.

Second, it doesn't help to hear words (directions, suggestions, orders, comments) and then fail to think about their meaning. Unless you understand what you hear and relate it to yourself, fix its meaning in your mind, you are wasting time and causing trouble. Hearing without understanding is somewhat like "looking" at something but not "seeing" it. Also, if you don't really comprehend what you are being told, it's up to you to fire questions until you do. Good listening requires you to use your ears—and your mind.

Finally, after you've heard and understood an order, direction, or suggestion, you must respond. If you don't want to act because you think what you've been told doesn't make sense or won't work, then tactfully argue it out. But after agreement has been reached, do something. Pick up the cue and follow the agreed-upon action. You can lose a job or fail to get ahead because of not "following" instructions. Good listening brings together your ears, mind, hands, feet, and body.

The author is not a medical specialist, and therefore no mention has been made of the possibility that you may have an actual hearing difficulty. If you follow the suggestions made in this chapter and still can't seem to grasp what you think you are hearing, it may be that something is wrong with your hearing apparatus.

Hundreds of thousands of school children find out each year that something is amiss with their hearing functions. It's possible that all of your working life you have been missing something of what's said in your presence just because your ears are faulty. If you suspect this is the situation, it would be an excellent investment of time and money to have your ears checked by a specialist. Most physicians are equipped to test you. If you wish, you can secure an appointment with a medical person with the formidable title of "otorhinolaryngologist," which means an individual specializing in diseases and functions of the ear, nose, and throat.

Speech is a mirror of the soul. As a man speaks, so is he.
Publius Syrus

CHAPTER 10

Watch Out for These No-No's

The eight chapters following this one deal with several hundred words, expressions, and kinds of sentences that you should avoid while talking your way to a better job. Before you plunge into them, give some thought to the few *worst* errors many people make most often.

The unacceptable and substandard no-no's in this chapter are those that will most quickly and surely cause others to fault the way you talk. The list is based upon many hours of listening to the way hundreds of people actually spoke in the street, on buses and trains, at various meetings, in social gatherings, in offices and restaurants, and over television and the radio.

The list does not begin to cover all the faulty talk that goes on (following chapters come close to doing this), but it does give you an overall view of those nonstandard items you should get rid of as quickly as possible. Having mastered these glaring mistakes, you can then go on to Chapters 11–18.

First, let's find out how much you know about standard and nonstandard usage. Would you speak as people did who were overheard making these remarks while this book was being written?

1. I'm in the center of this here picture; that's Betty next to the end.
2. Are you going to meet Joe and myself tonight?
3. When you finished the job, who did you ask to look at what you had done?
4. Jim stutters so badly that I can't hardly understand him.

5. The coffee shop is crowded; there's ten people waiting for seats.
6. He ain't going to pay the bill.
7. Between you and I, the food at that place is too highly seasoned.
8. He does not like any of them suits on sale.
9. If Jack don't come soon, he will miss the bus.
10. That conductor she should talk more slowly.
11. Everyone should watch out for their own personal belongings.
12. Dave asked me who he should give the money to.
13. Sue and me were not invited to the party.
14. When we arrived, the plane had already went.
15. He hated everything and everybody which caused him to lose his job.
16. You should of told me that you were coming.
17. Judy is a real good office manager.
18. Either the operators or the foreman are to blame for what happened.
19. The supervisor tried hard to learn me filing, but I couldn't understand it at all.
20. You have the right to invite whoever you wish.

Each of these 20 sentences contain an actual error of some sort or a usage that is considered by some to be inaccurate or incorrect. If you know what these mistakes (or expressions considered in bad form) are, if you are certain that you would never make them, then you can safely skip the remainder of this chapter. But if every one of the sentences sounds all right to you, then pay attention. (And refer to the end of this chapter where the mistakes are listed and corrected.)

The quality and so-called correctness of speech varies from job to job, office to office, and industry to industry. But no matter what work you do or where you do it, someone is certain to "put you down" if you use no-no's. Unfortunately, that someone may be a person who can raise your pay, recommend you for a better job, or suggest your firing. Errors in using words and phrases occur countless times every day. Nail down the following list of pitfalls before you go any further and take a long step toward more effective speech.

a, an

The choice between *a* and *an* depends on the beginning sound of the word that follows. *An* should be used before an initial vowel sound (a,e,i,o,u). *A* should appear before a word starting with a consonant sound (all letters of the alphabet that are not vowels).

Say *a* battery, *a* desk, *a* telephone, *a* voice. Say *an* apple, *an* ear, *an* import, *an* obligation, *an* umpire. *An* is hardly ever used incorrectly for *a*, but *a* is often used when *an* should be. Don't tag yourself as illiterate by saying "*a* answer," "*a* easy job," "*a* inch," "*a* opportunity," or "*a* unkind remark."

ain't

Many informed, educated persons use this word, but if you say it at work, you can be sure that someone who hears you will consider you subpar in speech. If you don't use *ain't* at any time—not even in relaxed talks with close friends and family members—you will not have to get rid of a hard-to-break habit. Instead of *ain't* say "isn't," or "is not," or "aren't," or "are not."

anywheres

Drop the "s." Say *anywhere*. In acceptable speech there is no such word as "anywheres."

Be

This little word meaning "to exist" or "to live" causes a lot of trouble. Explaining its various uses might be confusing, so just watch out for the following:

Say "you were," not "you was."
Say "you are," not "you be" or "you is."
Say "he is," "she is," "it is," not "he (she, it) be."
Say "we are," not "we be," "we am," "we was," or "we is."
Say "they are," not "they be" or "they is."

between you and I

Don't worry about the grammar that says prepositions (like *between*) are followed by the objective case. Just don't ever say "between you and I." It is never correct. Say "between you and *me*."

brung

This is one of the several verbs whose parts cause trouble; "I *brang* you a present" and "I *brung* you a present" are both substandard. The only acceptable forms are "bring" and "brought." Say "I *bring* you a present," "I *brought* you a present," and "I *have brought* you a present." No such word as "brang" (or "brung") is in the language.

da, dat, dem, dose

Using these forms for "the," "that," "them," and "those" is never allowable. Always make the "th" sound.

disregardless

Not everyone who hears you say "disregardless" will put you down as slovenly and uninformed. But some people will, because there is no such word in the language. Say "regardless" or "without regard."

done

This word is a form of the verb "do." Say "I do," "you do," "he does," "she does," "it does," "we do," "you do," "they do." Never say "I *done* it," "you *done* it," "he *done* it," "we *done* it," or "they *done* it." *Done* can never be used by itself. It must be used only with "has" or "have": "She has done it," "He has done it," "They have done it."

don't, doesn't

Don't is a short form of "do not." *Doesn't* is a short form of "does not." Use *doesn't* with "he," "she," or "it": "He *doesn't* want to work." Never use *doesn't* with *I, you, we,* or *they.* These are no-no's:

He *don't* want the money.
We *doesn't* want the money.
They *doesn't* like their new car.

don't have nothing

This is a double negative, two negative terms (*don't, nothing*) in the same statement. Such expressions are often considered illiterate. Don't run the risk of being considered a substandard speaker by making such remarks as

I *don't* have *nothing* to do with it. (Say "don't have *anything*.")
We *didn't* see *nobody* at the store. (Say "didn't see *anyone*.")
She *didn't* get *none*. (Say "didn't get *any*.")
I *couldn't* find my friend *nowhere*. (Say "*anywhere*.")

drunk

This troublesome verb may cause you to say something like "It tasted good, so I drunk it." Drink if you please, but never say "I drunk." Say "I drink" or "I drank." If you use *drunk*, add a word: "I *have drunk*."

each are

"Each of us *are* going" is the kind of remark that will raise someone's eyebrows. The words *each, anyone*, and *nobody* are singular (meaning "one") and should be followed by a singular verb. Say "Each of us *is* going." Say "Anyone in his right mind *knows* that"; "Nobody *was* there."

each, their

Each refers to "one," *their* to "more than one." Don't say "*Each* of us likes *their* jobs." Say "*Each* of us likes *his* job" or "*her* job."

feel badly

Badly means "harmfully," "inefficiently." Don't say "I feel *badly*" unless you mean that your sense of touch is inefficient.

Say "I feel bad" because *bad* means "not as it should be." If "I feel bad" doesn't sound right to you, say "I feel ill" or "I feel sick."

free gratis

This expression, commonly used by educated and uneducated speakers alike, is both wordy and inexact. *Gratis* means "for nothing," "without charge," "freely." Say *free* or *gratis* but don't use both in the same phrase.

good, well

Don't worry about which of these is an adjective (*good*) and which is both adjective and adverb (*well*). Just never make such statements as

That dinner surely tasted *well*. (Say *good*.)
The team played *good* during the first half. (Say *well*.)
He did *good* on the job. (Say *well*.)

hadn't ought

Say "I shouldn't go," not "I hadn't ought to go." *Hadn't ought* should never be used. Also, *should* is preferable to "had ought": "I *should* go there soon" (not "had ought to").

he, him

Don't concern yourself about case in grammar; just never make such statements as these:

Him and *me* are friends. (Say "He and I are friends.")
Me and *him* work together. (Say "He and I work together.")
What you say applies only to *he* and *me*. (Say "him and me.")

hisn, hern

No such words appear in any acceptable dialect. Say *his* and *hers*.

how come

This wordy expression is a sure sign of uneducated speech:

"*How come* you think that?" should read "*Why do* you think that?" Substitute *why* for *how come* in a sentence such as "She didn't know *how come* she was either hired or fired."

irregardless

This is an illiteracy, a blend of "irrespective" and "regardless." Never use it.

is

This form of the verb "to be" is often misused in substandard speech. It may help you to use it correctly if you can remember that it is singular (one); third person (used only with *he, she,* or *it*); and is in the present tense (now). Avoid such expressions as

Is you going with me? (Say "*Are* you going with me?")
You are right and I *is* wrong. (Say "I *am* wrong.")
They *is* not my friends. (Say "They *are* not my friends.")
Yesterday I *is* too sick to work. (Say "Yesterday I *was* too . . .)

John he

There are fancy grammatical terms for the practice of using more words than are needed, but all you need to remember is never to make such comments as "*John he* is my friend" and "My *sister she* lives in an apartment." Neither "he" nor "she" is needed in such sentences. Drop the italicized words from "My shopmates *they*" and "My brothers and I *we*."

lay, lie

As a verb, *lay* means "to place," "to cause to lie":
Lay it on the table.
Be careful when you *lay* the baby in her crib.
Trouble and confusion arise, however, because *lay* is a form of the verb *lie*, meaning "to recline," "to be or remain in a prostrate position: "When I am tired, I like to *lie* down and rest." When the action refers to past time, the form of *lie* is *lay*: "I *lay* down early last night." Study these uses:

The tools *laying* there are mine. (Say "lying.")
If you feel ill, *lay* down. (Say "lie.")
As I was *laying* there, the doorbell rang. (Say "lying.")
Lie your lunch basket on the table. (Say "lay.")
The cook *lied* my dinner in the oven. (Say "laid.")

learn, teach

Learn means "to gain knowledge." *Teach* means "to instruct," "to impart knowledge." You can *learn* something yourself, but you cannot *learn* anyone else anything. Never say "*Learn* me how to do that." Instead of *learn* say "teach," "instruct," "tell," or "show."

leave, let

The principal meanings of *leave* are "to go away from" and "to cause to remain": "She will *leave* here today." "*Leave* me alone so I can read." *Let* has a primary meaning of "allow" or "permit": "*Let* me do that for you." When the word "alone" is used, either "let" or "leave" is correct: "*Leave* (or let) Winnie alone." Don't make these mistakes:
Leave me do that job for you. (Say "let.")
When you go, *let* the door unlocked. (Say "leave.")
Please *leave* me wash the dishes tonight. (Say "let.")

me and you

Me and you is not acceptable English as the subject of a verb. It is also not polite wording. Reverse word order and say "you and me" as the object of a verb or preposition and "you and I" as the subject of a verb. These are correct statements:
Let's *you* and *I* go to the movies.
Will the bus wait for *you* and *me*?

nowheres

Like *anywheres, nowheres* is a never-to-be-used word. Drop the "s." "My gloves were nowhere to be found." "I couldn't find him *nowheres*" is wrong on two counts; it's a double negative and has the unwanted "s": say "I couldn't find him *anywhere*" or "I could find him *nowhere*."

of, have

Because in everyday speech most of us run words together, "could have," for instance, sounds like "could of." But *of* is not a verb. It's all right to say "could've," but it's damaging to say "I *could of* gone yesterday" or "You *could of* lent me the money."

Might of is like *could of*. Say "might have."

see, seen

The verb "to see" has as its present tense the form *see*. The past tense is *saw*. The past participle is *seen*: I *see* you now. I *saw* you yesterday. I have *seen* you every day this week. Just about everyone who hears you say the following will "put you down":

I *seen* him do it. (Say "saw.")
You never *seen* such a sight. (Say "saw.")
You've never *saw* such a sight in your life. (Say "seen.")

set, sit

Sit has a basic meaning of "to place oneself" and never requires an object. *Set* usually requires an object and means "to put," "to place." These usages are standard:

Set the basket on the table and *sit* down.

I *sat* in my room all day (not *set*).

Your friend is *sitting* in the car (not *setting*).

Is is, however, correct to refer to the "setting" sun and to a "setting" or "sitting" hen.

somewheres

This is an "uneducated," illiterate word. Don't use it, not ever. Drop the "s."

that there

Both "that" and "there" are acceptable words, but they should never be used together. It's a dead giveaway to refer to "that there machine" or "that there" anything. It's all right to refer to "that machine there," but always keep something between the words. The same recommendation applies to "this here." Omit "here" in a statement such as "*This here* locker is mine." Or say "This locker here is mine."

theirselves

There is no such word as *theirselves*. Use "themselves" in a sentence such as "They hurt *theirselves* trying to put out the fire."

them, them there

Never use "them" for "these" or "those." Don't say "*Them* people bother me"; say "these" or "those." (It's all right to use *them* as the object of a verb: The manager likes *them*.) "Them there" is as much to be avoided as "that there." Drop "there" or put a word in between "them" and "there."

there is, there are

Use *there is* when what follows refers to only one person or one object or one event. Say *there are* when what comes next refers to more than one:

There *is* (not *are*) a good reason for my action.
There *are* (not *is*) three letters missing.

The same rule applies to "there was" and "there were"; to "has been" and "have been"; to "seem" and "seems"; and several other similar verbs.

was, were

Don't give yourself away by misusing these parts of the verb "to be." Don't worry about the grammar of mood and number involved; just don't say

There *was* fifty of us in the room. (Say "were.")
There *were* only one of us ready to leave. (Say "was.")
If I *was* you, I'd quit. (Say "were.")

we, us

Again, forget about the grammar of case. Don't ever say such sentences as these:

They gave the tickets to *we* workers. (Say "us.")

Us employees then went on strike. (Say "we.")

Stores want *we* customers to pay our bills promptly. (Say "us.")

Your crew and then *us* will start soon. (Say "we.")

who, whom

No situation in English speech causes more difficulty for more persons than choosing between *who* and *whom* (and *whoever, whomever* when they are used). Current usage studies indicate that the distinction between these forms is breaking down, because keeping them straight is difficult and because you may begin a remark with *who*, not knowing how you are going to end the statement. Because most people consider *whom* less natural than *who*, they often use *who* even when *whom* is indicated.

The grammatical rule is simple: use *who* (or *whoever*) as the subject of a verb or as a predicate pronoun. Use *whom* (*whomever*) as the object of a verb or preposition.

1. The question of *who* can go is unimportant. (Here, *who* is the subject of "can go." The entire clause, "who can go," is the object of the preposition *of*.)
2. This is the fireman *whom* we saw on top of the building. (Here, *whom* is the object of "saw.")
3. He asked me *who* I thought would be elected. (The case of a pronoun depends upon its use and should not be influenced by words that come between it and its antecedent. Check this sentence by omitting *I thought*. *Who* is then seen to be the subject of "would be elected.")
4. My son danced with the girl *whom* everyone suspected the committee had chosen Beauty Queen. (Here, check by omitting "everyone suspected.")

When doubtful, substitute *he* or *him* for *who* or *whom* to arrive at a decision:

1. Who/whom are you voting for? (For who/whom are you voting? He/him are you voting for? For he/him are you voting?)

2. This is the kind of public servant who/whom we need.
   . . . we need who/whom.
   . . . we need he/him.

Don't skip quickly over these 40 no-no's. Chances are that you sometimes slip. And when you do, you may lessen your chances for getting ahead.

And here are the errors in the 20 sentences given at the beginning of this chapter:

1. Omit *here*
2. *me*, not *myself*
3. *whom*, not *who*
4. *can hardly*, not *can't hardly*
5. *there are*, not *there's*
6. *is not*, *isn't*, not *ain't*
7. *me*, not *I*
8. *those*, not *them*
9. *doesn't*, not *don't*
10. omit *he*
11. *his* (or her) not *their*
12. *whom*, not *who*
13. *I*, not *me*
14. *gone*, not *went*
15. *who*, not *which*
16. *have*, not *of*
17. *really*, not *real*
18. *is*, not *are*
19. *teach*, not *learn*
20. *whomever*, not *whoever*

CHAPTER 11

Confusing Look-Alikes and Sound-Alikes

Standard words can be misused just as can be substandard ones. If an acceptable word is given an incorrect meaning or is made to perform a job it should not have, what results is an error in usage sometimes called an *impropriety*. For instance, *eats* is a proper verb (he *eats* three times a day), but using the word as a noun (he likes good *eats*) is usually considered improper. Glaring examples of improper, substandard use of words given in the preceding chapter include "this here," "that there," "hadn't ought," "don't" for "doesn't," "sit" for "set," and "of" for "have."

It's all too easy to use a word which resembles another in looks or sound but which doesn't say exactly what is meant. Hundreds of such confusing "pairs" exist in English. Also, through carelessness, ignorance, or confusion you may mistake one word for another even when they don't sound alike or look alike but do have some sort of "paired" meaning or association. In improving your speech, try to avoid mixing up such often-confused words as these:

ability, capacity.

Ability means the power to do something, mental or physical ("ability to manage an office"). *Capacity* is the ability to hold, contain, or absorb ("a suitcase filled to capacity").

accept, except.

Accept means "to receive" or "to say yes to"; *except* means "to exclude" or "to exempt." ("I accept the terms of this contract." "Jim was excepted from the general invitation.") As a preposition, *except* means "other than." ("No one except me knew the combination.")

affect, effect.

Affect, as a verb, means "to assume," or "to influence." ("Her voice affected me strangely.") *Effect*, as a verb, means "to cause"; as a noun, it means "result." ("Being foreman effected a change in his attitude." "The decision had a profound effect on labor relations.")

among, between.

The former indicates a relationship of more than two objects; *between* refers to only two, or to more than two when each object is considered in relation to the others. ("The rivalry between Joe and Sam is intense." "Trade between nations is desirable." "The land was divided among five heirs."

complement, compliment.

Complement means something which completes. ("That hat will complement your wardrobe.") A *compliment* is a flattering comment. ("When she remarked that he was handsome, Ted thanked her for the compliment.")

continual, continuous.

In some uses, these words are synonymous. A distinction is that *continual* implies "a close recurrence in time," in "rapid succession"; *continuous* implies "without interruption." ("I objected most to my sister's continual quarreling." "The continuous dripping of water from that leaky faucet unnerved me.")

convince, persuade.

Convince means to satisfy the understanding of someone about the truth of a situation or statement: "Marie convinced me by quoting exact figures." *Persuade* means, or suggests, winning over someone to a course of action or belief, perhaps by an appeal to reason or good sense: "Joy persuaded her husband to consult a lawyer."

emigrate, immigrate.

The former means "to leave"; the latter means "to enter." ("Our foreman *emigrated* from Russia in 1948." "In the future, a greater number of people from the Latin countries will *immigrate* to the United States.")

farther, further.

These are interchangeable; however, prefer *farther* to indicate "space," "a measurable distance," and *further* to indicate "greater in quantity, degree, or time," and also "moreover," "in addition to." ("I drove eight miles farther." "Let us give the matter further consideration.")

former, latter.

Former applies to the first of two in a series. When you refer to the first of three or more, say *first* or *first-named*. In the sense in which it contrasts with *former*, *latter* refers to the second of two things mentioned. When referring to the last of three or more, say *last-named*, not *latter*.

funeral, funereal.

Funeral (FYOO.nuhr.uhl) means "burial rites." *Funereal* (Fyoo.NEER.i.uhl) means "sad," "doleful," and "gloomy." "At the funeral of her friend, Polly's face was funereal."

gourmand, gourmet.

These words have to do with eating, but they are different in meaning. A *gourmand* is a large eater. ("Teen-age boys are notorious gourmands.") A *gourmet* is a fastidious eater, an epicure. ("Les Chevaliers du Tastevin is an association of well-known gourmets.")

hang, hung.

The principal parts of *hang* are *hang, hung, hung*. However, when the word refers to the death penalty, the parts are *hang, hanged, hanged.* ("The pictures are hung." "The murderer was hanged.")

healthful, healthy.

These words are often used interchangeably, but *healthful* means "conducive to health"; *healthy* means "possessing health." In other words, places and foods are healthful, people and animals are healthy. ("An athlete must be a healthy person because of healthful daily workouts.")

human, humane.

The term *human* refers to a person. Some writers and speakers do not use the word alone to refer to man as man; they say or write "human being." However, use of the word alone as a noun has a long and respectable background. *Humane* means "tender," "merciful," "considerate," ("The general insisted upon humane treatment of all prisoners.")

impractical, impracticable.

Distinctions in the meanings of these words have broken down somewhat, but the former means "not practical" or "speculative" or "theoretically." *Impracticable* means "not capable of being used," "unmanageable." ("His plan is impractical and his instructions are impracticable.")

jealous, zealous.

The former means "resentful" or "envious" and should be followed by *of*, not *for*. ("Ingrid is jealous of Margaret's ring.") *Zealous* means "diligent," "devoted." ("They were zealous workers on behalf of their candidate.")

later, latter.

The spelling of these words is often confused. They also have different meanings. *Later* refers to time. ("The train arrived five minutes later than usual." *Latter* means "the second of two" ("I prefer the latter choice.")

lead, led.

These words show the confusion that our language suffers because of using different symbols to represent one sound. *Lead* (pronounced *leed*) is the present tense of the verb and causes little or no difficulty. *Led* (pronounced lehd) is the past tense and is often misspelled with *ea*. ("Lead the horse around the paddock." "He led the horse around the paddock yesterday.")

least, lest.

The former means "smallest." "slightest." The latter means "for fear that." ("It was the very *least* I could do." "Close the door *lest* our secret be overheard.")

loan, lend.

Many careful speakers use *loan* only as a noun ("to make a loan") and *lend* as a verb ("to lend money"). Because of constant and widespread usage, *loan* is now considered a legitimate verb to be avoided only in strictly formal English.

luxuriant, luxurious.

The former term refers to abundant growth; *luxurious* pertains to luxury. ("The blooms in her garden were *luxuriant*." "Silk curtains gave the simple room a *luxurious* touch.")

marital, martial.

Marital refers to marriage; *martial* refers to war. Only cynics would maintain that the words are interchangeable. Note the spellings and pronunciations: MAR.uh.tul and MAHR.shuhl.

most, almost.

Most is the superlative of *many* and *much* and means "greatest in amount, quality, or degree." *Almost* indicates "very nearly," "all but." Most is colloquial when used for almost. ("He has almost (not most) come to a decision.")

party, person.

Party implies or suggests a group and, except in legal and telephonic language, should not be used to refer to one person:

We invited a hundred persons to the *party*. He is the *person* (not party) to whom you referred. As nouns, *individual* and *person* mean the same thing.

phenomenon, phenomena.

The former is singular (meaning "one"); the latter is plural (meaning "more than one"). *This* phenomenon *is* hard to understand. *These* phenomena *are* hard to understand. *Phenomenons* is a permissible but not preferred substitute for *phenomena*. Note the pronunciations: fi.NOM.i.non and fi.NOM.i.nah.

precede, proceed.

These words have different pronunciations and meanings. *Precede* (pre.SEED) means to come before, to go in advance of. *Proceed* (PRO.seed) means to go forward, to carry on. The designer preceded her staff into the room and proceeded to drape the model.

quiet, quit, quite.

Quiet means "still" or "calm." ("Later, at a quiet meeting in the board room, he announced his resignation.") *Quit* means "to stop," "to desist." ("He quit his complaining.") *Quite* means "positively," "entirely." ("You are quite sure of your facts?")

rang, wrung.

Rang is the past tense of the verb *ring*, meaning "to give forth a sound." ("I rang the bell and then entered.") *Wrung* is the past tense of the verb *wring*, "to press or squeeze." ("I wrung the water from my socks.") *Rung* is a principal part of the verb *ring*: "She has rung the bell for an hour."

regard, regards.

The latter is used with *as* to mean "consider" or "think." ("He regards me as a sister.") *In regard to* and *with regard to* are idiomatically sound, but both phrases are wordy. Limit your use of *regards* to the plural form of the noun *regard* and the singular form of the verb. ("Please give your aunt my regards.")

sensual, sensuous.

The first refers to gratification of bodily pleasures or appetites. *Sensuous* suggests the appeal of that which is pleasing to the senses. ("The movie served no purpose other than to arouse sensual desires." "The velvet had a sensuous softness.")

some, somewhat.

The former is an adjective, as in "some money" and "some fruit." *Somewhat* means "to some degree," "to some extent": The patient is somewhat (not some) better today. *Some* is informal and even slangy when used to mean "exceptional" or "remarkable": "He is some player" makes sense but is considered faulty diction.

statue, stature, statute.

A *statue* is a sculptured likeness. ("A statue of General Grant may be found in the park.") *Stature* is often used figuratively. ("She has great political stature.") *A statute* is a law. ("This statute is unenforceable and should be stricken from the book.")

tasteful, tasty.

The former means "having or showing good taste, sense, or judgment." Tasty means "flavorful," "savory," "having the quality of tasting good." ("She made a tasteful arrangement of linen, china, and silverware. It was her tasty casserole of veal, however, that won first prize.")

then, than.

These words are often confused in pronunciation. *Than* is a conjunction used in clauses of comparison. ("I made a better score than Harvey did.") *Then* is an adverb of time. ("You may then proceed to clean up.")

till, until, 'til.

Both *till* and *until* mean "before," "up to," and "when." Use either one you please; both are acceptable. *'Til* is a shortened form of *until* and is usually considered poetic or old-fashioned. "Until (or *till*, never *'til*) you pay me what you owe, I can't leave."

unmoral, amoral, immoral.

Unmoral means "having no morality," "non-moral," "unable to distinguish right from wrong." Thus an infant or a mentally disordered person is unmoral. *Amoral* means "not concerned with moral standards," "not to be judged by criteria or standards of morality." Morons and animals, for example, may be called amoral. *Immoral* means "wicked," "contrary to accepted principles of right and wrong." The acts of thieves, murderers, and embezzlers may be called immoral.

unpractical, impractical, impracticable.

The first two of these terms are interchangeable, although *impractical* is considered more formal and refined. Each means "not practical." "lacking practical usefulness or wisdom." *Impracticable* means "not capable of being carried out, used, or managed." ("It is impractical to suggest that a boy be sent on a man's errand." "Because of the high wind, our leaf-raking methods were impracticable.")

weather, whether.

Carelessness in saying *whether* results in a pronunciation close to that of *weather*. *Whether* means "in case" and "if it be that": "She will soon leave whether you do or not." *Weather* refers to climate: "What's the weather forecast for tomorrow?"

MORE PAIRS THAT SNARE

Now that you see how easy it is to misuse a word, to mistake one word for another, go a step further. (The preceding list covers only a fraction of the words that cause trouble.) Select a few words that you frequently say or read and look them up in a dictionary to make certain they express exactly what you have in mind. Are there some look-alikes or sound-alikes that you should be using instead?

For example, do you ever use "reported" when you mean "reputed"? "Reported" means "made known": The crime was reported to the police. "Reputed" means "supposed": She is *reputed* to be an excellent executive. Or do you say "venal" when what you really mean is "venial"? *Venal* means "for sale," "corrupt." *Venial* means "excusable," "pardonable." A venal sin is a big one, a venial sin is less damaging. If you associate *venial* with "genial" and *venal* with "penal," confusion will disappear.

Take your time, think, and consult a dictionary as you examine the following list of paired words. Try to learn their meanings so as never to say one when you mean the other. (True, some of these "pairs that snare" will cause problems in spelling more than in pronunciation.) Having learned through this exercise how tricky words can be, watch out for others in your talk and reading.

accede, exceed

access, excess

adapt, adopt

advice, advise

advise, inform

allusion, illusion

amount, number

anecdote, antidote

angel, angle

assure, ensure (insure)

beside, besides

breath, breathe

censor, censure

chafe, chaff

clench, clinch

complementary,
   complimentary

device, devise

disinterested, uninterested

dairy, diary

decent, descent (dissent)

desert, dessert

emigrant, immigrant

eminent, imminent

envelop, envelope

expect, suspect

foreword, forward

flaunt, flout

genius, genus

ingenious, ingenuous

loose, lose

moral, morale

personal, personnel

prescribe, proscribe

raise, rise
respectfully, respectively
stimulant, stimulus

through, thorough
your, you're

EXERCISE

With the help of your dictionary, select the more suitable of the two italicized words in each of the following sentences:

1. The supervisor said she left early because she wasn't feeling *good well*.
2. If you do that you are *liable apt* to get caught.
3. This basket will hold *fewer less* apples than that one.
4. The acts of rapists and murderers are *unmoral immoral*.
5. Jessie said that she was determined to go *anyway anyways*.
6. If they don't hurry *they're their* going to miss the bus.
7. Jack feels *bad badly* about not keeping his promise.
8. The orders given were *verbal oral*, not written.
9. Joan quickly ate the *remainder balance* of her meal.
10. Rose and Ted have a *common mutual* dislike for each other.

CHAPTER 12

Watch Out for Tricky Verbs

You learned in grammar school that a verb is a word that "says something." A verb expresses action of some kind or, if not action, a kind of existence: to talk, walk, sleep, live, die, breathe, and speak. But knowing this much about verbs helps very little in learning how to use them properly. Problems arise because verbs have four forms (infinitive, present tense, past tense, and past participle); voice (active and passive); mood (indicative, imperative, and subjunctive); and six different tenses. But you can skip over most such matters because the real trouble-maker in using verbs is their principal parts.

In almost every language, verbs have principal parts. English and German have three; French, Spanish, and Italian have five. The principal parts of an English verb are its (1) present tense or present infinitive; (2) past tense; and (3) past participle. A helpful plan to fix these parts in mind is to substitute those of any verb in these sentences:

I *walk* today.
I *walked* yesterday.
I *have walked* every day this week.

Verbs "form" their principal parts in several different ways, but all you need to do is to put them into the expressions just given. If your "ear" tells you that you have them right, good. If not, look in your dictionary where principal parts of many verbs are listed.

You can probably use most verbs with ease, but just in case you can't, what follows are the principal parts of the most troublesome verbs in the English language. Study them carefully if you need to, memorize them, put each of them into the expressions previously mentioned. Whatever you do, get them right. More errors are made in using verbs than in any other single area of the language. You can't talk your way to a better job unless and until you know the principal parts of verbs.

arise	arose	arisen
ask	asked	asked
attack	attacked	attacked
awake	awoke	awakened
bear	bore	borne (born: given birth to)
beat	beat	beaten
become	became	become
begin	began	begun
bid (auction)	bid	bid
bid (command)	bade, bid	bidden, bid
bite	bit	bitten, bit
bleed	bled	bled
blow	blew	blown
break	broke	broken
bring	brought	brought
broadcast	broadcast, broadcasted	broadcast, broadcasted
build	built	built
burn	burned, burnt	burned, burnt
burst	burst	burst
buy	bought	bought
cast	cast	cast
catch	caught	caught
choose	chose	chosen
come	came	come
cut	cut	cut
deal	dealt	dealt
dig	dug	dug

do	did	done
draw	drew	drawn
dream	dreamed, dreamt	dreamed, dreamt
dress	dressed, drest	dressed, drest
drink	drank	drunk, drunken (see dictionary)
drive	drove	driven
dwell	dwelt, dwelled	dwelt, dwelled
eat	ate	eaten
fall	fell	fallen
feel	felt	felt
fight	fought	fought
find	found	found
flow	flowed	flowed
fly	flew	flown
fly (baseball)	flied	flied
forbid	forbade, forbad	forbidden
forget	forgot	forgotten, forgot
forsake	forsook	forsaken
freeze	froze	frozen
get	got	got, gotten
give	gave	given
go	went	gone
grow	grew	grown
happen	happened	happened
have	had	had
hear	heard	heard
help	helped	helped
hit	hit	hit
hurt	hurt	hurt
keep	kept	kept
know	knew	known
lay	laid	laid
lead	led	led
learn	learned, learnt	learned, learnt
leave	left	left
lend	lent	lent
let	let	let

lie (falsehood)	lied	lied
loose	loosed	loosed
lose	lost	lost
make	made	made
mean	meant	meant
pass	passed	passed, past
pay	paid	paid
prejudice	prejudiced	prejudiced
prove	proved	proved, proven
put	put	put
raise	raised	raised
read	read	read
ride	rode	ridden
rise	rose	risen
run	ran	run
say	said	said
see	saw	seen
sell	sold	sold
set	set	set
shake	shook	shaken
shine	shone	shone
show	showed	shown, showed
sing	sang	sung
sink	sank	sunk
sit	sat	sat
sling	slung	slung
smell	smelled, smelt	smelled, smelt
speak	spoke	spoken
spell	spelled, spelt	spelled, spelt
spoil	spoiled, spoilt	spoiled, spoilt
spring	sprang, sprung	sprung
stand	stood	stood
steal	stole	stolen
strike	struck	struck, stricken
strive	strove, strived	striven, strived
swear	swore	sworn
swim	swam	swum
take	took	taken

teach	taught	taught
tell	told	told
think	thought	thought
throw	threw	thrown
use	used	used
wake	waked, woke	waked, woken
work	worked, wrought	worked, wrought
write	wrote	written

Check up on yourself. Have you really learned these principal parts? For each of the following 10 sentences, select the correct form of the verb appearing in parentheses. If necessary, study the list again.

A

1. She had apparently (drink) both bottles.
2. Marvin did not look like someone who had (swim) the Channel, and he didn't.
3. The day the water mains (burst), we irrigated our tomatoes.
4. It was Eustace: he had (take) the plane from the hangar.
5. Had he only (bear) a little more to the left he would have hit the water.
6. The sailor caught the line and was (cast) onto the lobster boat.
7. Just then someone (begin) to pull rabbits out of the hat.
8. His father's spirits (sink) when Bill declined the offer.
9. I fear, Dawson, that you have (draw) the shorter straw.
10. Who knows how long this jet has (fly) in the wrong direction?

B

Name the appropriate form of the verb that appears in parentheses in each of these sentences:

1. Don't ever think that she (forget) your birthday last year.
2. Has this team ever (win) the league championship?
3. She saw that my favorite painting was (hang) in the room.
4. Milly claimed that the telephone had (ring) more than ten times.
5. We saw her (lay) the envelope on the bed.
6. Ned missed the show because he had (lie) in bed all afternoon.
7. The quartet (sing) several of its most popular songs.
8. The worried parents stood there, (wring) their hands.
9. When the President entered the room, all of us (rise) to greet him.
10. Jock soon realized that he had (lose) his audience.

C

For each numbered part of the following sentences, select a letter to indicate the standard verb form.

1. I was (A. struck; B. stricken) by the fact that all three
2. had been (A. born; B. borne) the same month of the year.
3. After his fall he (A. shook; B. shaked; C. shaken) his head to clear it,
4. then (A. stand; B. stood) up
5. and (A. ask; B. asked) each of us
6. what we thought had (A. happen; B. happened).
7. We (A. use; B. used) to try the south end of the lake every morning;
8. sometimes we (A. try; B. tried) for northern pike off the deep bank
9. and occasionally (A. come; B. came) up with a large one,
10. but usually we (A. catched; B. caught) only a few pan fish.

D

Give the three principal parts of each of the following verbs. If you are stuck, consult your dictionary. (If the principal parts are not given there, perhaps illustrative sentences in the definitions will provide clues.)

hide	spin
seek	sting
shrink	tear
slay	wear

CHAPTER 13

How's Your Idiom?

The word *idiom* comes from a Greek term meaning "individual," "peculiar," or "private." An idiom is an expression in a language, dialect, or style of speaking that is peculiar to a people such as the American, Spanish, or French peoples. Every language has its own peculiarities, terms and expressions whose meanings cannot always be learned from the usual meanings of the words they contain.

Acceptable idiomatic usage in the United States will give you little trouble if you are a native-born speaker of English. You constantly use idioms in the accepted, understandable ways you have heard since infancy. True, many of the idioms we employ every day may not "make sense," may violate grammatical rules, and may differ from the normal patterns of language. No matter. They are said and written by everyone everywhere and are universally accepted. Every standard idiom is familiar, deeprooted, and readily understandable.

But if English (American) is not your native tongue, idiomatic usage will raise many problems. Difficulties with idiom arise from (1) how you group words, (2) the order of words you use, and (3) the inflections (changes) in word form that should take place.

For instance, if your native language is French, you might be inclined to say "a house white" instead of "a white house." Why? Because in French you would say "un maison blanc." "It makes cold" might sound all right to you, because in French you would say "il fait froid." In American (English) idiom, only "it is cold" is acceptable.

What would a person whose native language is Italian make of the English idiom "every other day"? In Italian idiom the expression might be "un giórno si, un giórno no" (one day yes, one day no). The English idiom "step by step" in Italian would be "di grado in grado."

A Spanish-speaking person learning English might translate the sentence "Everyone was working" into "Todo el mundo trabajaba." Or one might say (in translation) "Here one speaks Spanish" instead of "Spanish is spoken here."

A person from Germany learning English might say "I have the old man already seen" because in German the idea would be expressed by "Ich habe den alten Mann gesehen." Or if a German heard the command "Open your books," he or she might mutter "Machen Sie die Bücher auf."

As a speaker of American English you might tell a foreigner not to say "many boy is," "a pupils," and "ten foot." You would utterly confuse him with such acceptable idiomatic usage as "many *a* boy is," "a *few* pupils," and "a ten-foot *pole*." Much correct idiomatic usage is indeed illogical.

One generalized statement about English idioms is that several words combined often lose their literal (exact) meaning and express something only remotely suggested by any one word: *bed of roses, birds of a feather, black list, dark horse, get even with, open house, read between the lines, toe the line, to strike a deal, to turn a corner, hot cup of coffee, to be your age, to take after one's mother, pretty blue ladies dress, take off for a vacation, to step into a job, many is the time, naked eye, to come in handy, to catch fire, to catch a cold, to talk one's ear off, petty cash, square dance, pilot plant, blue laws, flying saucer, walking papers.*

Another comment is that parts of the human body have suggested numerous idiomatic expressions: "burn one's fingers," "all thumbs," "rub elbows with," "step on someone's toes," "take to heart," "catch one's eye," "put one's foot in one's mouth," "bend one's ear," "with half an eye," "pay through the nose," "down in the mouth," and "have a leg to stand on."

A third generalization is that hundreds of idiomatic phrases are formed by various parts of speech combined with others in a haphazard way. For example, the same word can combine with others to form phrases that are quite different in meaning: make away with, make believe, make bold, make do, make fast, make for, make good, make merry, make out, make over, make ready, and make up.

An even more complex idiomatic situation involves "look":

look alive (be wide awake)
look after (minister to)
look back (review the past)
look daggers (stare angrily)
look down on (regard with scorn)
look for (seek, search)
look forward to (anticipate)
look in on (visit)

look on (observe)
look oneself (appear normal)
look out (be on guard)
look over (examine)
look sharp (be alert)
look to (give attention)
look up (refer to)
look up to (respect)

Still other examples are these:

accompanied	*by* others
	with grief
affinity	*of* persons or things
	between two persons or things
	with another person or thing
agree	*on* a plan
	with a person
	in a belief
analogous	*in* a quality
	to or *with* others
concerned	*for* someone or something
	in an undertaking
	with or *about* a subject or topic
contend	*for* a principle
	with an individual
	against an obstacle
differ	*with* a person
	from something else
	on, *over*, or *about* a question

impatient	*at* someone's conduct
	with someone else
	for something desired
	of restraint
rewarded	*with* a gift
	by a person
	for something done

Your speech at work and at home should conform to the idiomatic word combinations generally acceptable. Reliable dictionaries contain some explanations of idiomatic usage following words that require such detail, but the information provided is not always complete or clear.

Twenty idiomatic and unidiomatic expressions follow. They are representative of several hundred idioms that can cause genuine problems:

Idiomatic	**Unidiomatic**
accord with	accord to
according to	according with
acquaint with	acquaint to
adverse to	adverse against
aim to prove	aim at proving
among themselves	among one another
angry with (a person)	angry at (a person)
as regards	as regards to
authority on	authority about
cannot help talking	cannot help but talk
comply with	comply to
conform to, with	conform in
correspond to (a thing)	correspond with (a thing)
desirous of	desirous to
identical with	identical to
in accordance with	in accordance to
prefer (one) to (another)	prefer (one) over (another)
prior to	prior than
superior to	superior than
unequal to	unequal for

The following idiomatic expressions will serve as a checklist, containing as it does many of the most commonly used idioms in the English language:

abstain from
accede to
accommodate to
acquiesce in
acquit of
adapted to, from
addicted to
adept in
adhere to
adjacent to
admit to, of
advantage of, over
agreeable to
alien from, to
amused at, by, with
antidote for
apart from
append to
approve of
arrive at, in
assent to
associate with
assure of
averse to
basis of, for
blanket with
blasé about
blend with
boast of, about
border on, upon
capable of
careful of, with, about
caution against
characteristic of

coincide with
compare to (illustration)
compare with (examine)
compatible with
concur in, with
conducive to
confide in, to
confident of
connect by, with
consent to
consistent with
contemptuous of
convict of
cured of
deficient in
dependent on, upon
deprive of
derive from
desire for
desirous of
detract from
different from
disagree with
disdain for
disapprove of
dissatisfied with
dissent from
distinguish between, from
ejected from
emigrate from
empty of
endowed with
enter into, on, upon
envious of

essential to
estimated at
exclusive of
expert in
fascination for
fond of
fondness for
foreign to
free from, of
fugitive from
grateful to, for
guard against
hint at
hope for, of
impeach for, of
implicit in
imply by
inconsistent with
independent of
infer from
inferior to
infested with
initiate into
inseparable from
instruct in
intercede with, for
interfere with
isolate from
jealous of
jeer at
laugh at, over
live at, on, in
made from, out of, of
monopoly of
need for, of
negligent of, in
obedient to
object to

oblivious of
observant of
occupied by, with
opportunity for, of
originate in, with
overcome by, with
parallel to, with, between
part from, with
partial to
participate in
pay for, to, with
peculiar to
persevere in
pertinent to
pleased at, by, with
plunged in (despair)
plunged into (liquid)
preclude from
preferable to
pregnant by, with
preparatory to
prerequisite to (adjective)
prerequisite of (noun)
prior to
proficient in
profit by
prohibit from
protest against
provide with, for, against
punishable by
purge of, from
pursuit of
qualify for, as
question about, concerning,
   on, of
reason with (verb)
reason for (noun)
reconciled to, with

regret for, at
repugnant to
responsibility for
revel in
rich in
rid of
scared at, by
sensitive to
separate from
similar to
solution of, to
substitute for
suitable to, for, with

sympathize with
tamper with
tax with, for
thrill at, to, with
treat of (a topic)
treat with (an opponent)
unfavorable to, toward, for
unmindful of
vie with
worthy of
yearn for, after, toward
zealous in

Ease and confidence in using idiomatic expressions in any language is a sure sign of mastery of that language, whatever it is. To build your confidence, *study* the lists of idiomatic expressions given in this chapter. Listen carefully to capable speakers of English and try to model your speech on theirs, especially their use of expressions and phrases that seem strange to you. And before you leave this chapter, make sure that you can select the proper words to put into the blanks in these sentences:

A

1. Do not infer _____ my statements that I dislike you.
2. She was not desirous _____ running afoul of the law.
3. Stanley said he was not averse _____ the idea.
4. Gladys was admitted _____ the manager's office.
5. It is difficult to accommodate ourselves _____ that tight schedule.
6. I didn't agree _____ any such thing.
7. He will never comply _____ your request.
8. What do you imply _____ your remark?
9. Two hours prior _____ leaving, she opened the letter.
10. Marguerite tried to substitute cleverness _____ valid argument.
11. Eleanor is too concerned _____ your appearance.

12. I didn't think her capable _____ doing such a thing.
13. We are now reconciled _____ living in a small house.
14. I shall prohibit them _____ doing that.
15. Please don't interfere _____ our vacation plans.
16. Do you know an antidote _____ this poison?
17. They could not bear to part _____ the trophy.
18. Are we really dependent _____ your father?
19. He was then ejected _____ the theater.
20. Bill Curtis will pay you _____ the work.

B

For each of the following sentences select the preferred expression. Your ear, your common sense, and a dictionary should help you to choose the proper idiomatic usage.

1. The movie had a very different ending (A. than; B. to) the one we expected.
2. On (A. the; B. a) whole, we were pleased with the show.
3. For breakfast I prefer a cooked cereal (A. over; B. than; C. to) eggs and bacon.
4. The girl differed a good deal (A. from; B. with; C. to) what we had expected.
5. Bill said that he suffered (A. from; B. with) frequent headaches.
6. They saw him going (A. in; B. into) the drugstore an hour ago.
7. As (A. far as; B. for) buying the oil and gas, you can count on me.
8. She has an unusual ability (A. to make; B. for making) firm friends.
9. Jack says that he will be late and for us not to wait (A. on; B. for) him.
10. Sue finished medical school (A. at; B. on) the top of the class.

C

Give the generally accepted meanings of these idioms:

1. to stick to one's last
2. to put through the mill
3. to have too many irons in the fire
4. a chip off the old block
5. to have an axe to grind

D

Use the word *head* in idiomatic expressions meaning

1. to be intelligent
2. to talk and talk
3. to be conceited
4. to become excited
5. to get ahead

CHAPTER 14

Language and Slanguage

Of the 10,000-20,000 English words in the "average" American adult's vocabulary, slang makes up about 10%, between 1,000 and 2,000 words. If you use slang in only 10% of what you say, your speech cannot be seriously faulted. But if you count on slang to express many or most of your ideas and thoughts, you should watch out as you try to talk your way to greater success.

Yes, nearly everyone uses slang, but not everyone *overuses* it. The most effective speakers you know—usually persons who are "getting ahead" in one way or another—probably use less slang than you might have thought and usually have a specific purpose in mind when they do. It may be that you are not even aware that you use quantities of slang because what you hear every day sounds like the words and expressions you use yourself.

Just what is slang and what's good and bad about it? The term *slang* is a label for a kind of informal word use that ranges from outright illiteracies, vulgarity, obscenities, and profanity to acceptable shortened forms of words, clipped speech, novel expressions, and forced humor. Slang is also a group term for the kinds of language that go by the names of "cant," "jargon," and "argot."

Cant (one kind of slang) is the familiar, conversational idiom used by persons in a particular trade, occupation, class, age group, profession, or sect. *Jargon* is "shop talk," the vocabulary used in a certain field of work or activity. (Two recommendations: Never engage in shop talk with other than fellow-workers; when you do "talk shop," make certain that your hearers understand what you mean.) *Argot* is the jargon of some criminal group.

Thus, there is slang of the underworld, of narcotic addicts, of the financial world, of rock musicians, of tramps and hobos, of baseball players, of sports writers, of bartenders, of school and college students, of theatrical people, of railroad workers, of soda fountain employees, and of those in many other trades, occupations, and ways of life.

Most users of slang are trying for an easy, quick, highly personal way of speaking, a purpose no one can fault. Although slang comes from argot, cant, and jargon, some of it is easily understood and is widely accepted by the general public. Actually, some slang eventually becomes "standard" speech. Much slang, however, is never accepted and never appears in dictionaries even with a "caution" label. In fact, most slang has a short life, flourishing briefly and quickly dying out.

Why is slang popular and why do you and I use it every day in informal talk? Here are some reasons for its widespread use:

1. Slang often communicates more quickly, more personally, and more easily than so-called standard expressions.
2. It is frequently colorful and lively.
3. It provides helpful short cuts in expression.
4. It doesn't sound stiff, formal, or sentimental.
5. It is forceful partly because it is brief.

Even more reasons could be given for the popularity of slang. But slang also has its weaknesses. Among others, these may be cited:

1. Using slang words prevents a speaker from searching for the exact words needed to express meaning. Many slang expressions are only rubber stamps. To call someone a "swell guy" or a "lemon" or a "square" hardly expresses exactly or fully any real critical judgment or intelligent description. Instead, such words are more likely to convey

the speaker's own laziness, careless thinking, and poverty of vocabulary.

2. Slang is all right in its place, but it is frequently not in keeping with the context, what precedes and follows.

3. Slang may be colorful and humorous, but few slang expressions by themselves serve the purpose of conveying a clear and accurate message from speaker to listener.

4. Most slang words last for a brief time only and then pass out of use, becoming unintelligible to hearers.

WHERE SLANG COMES FROM

Slang appears in numerous forms. Many newly-coined words are slang: *hornswoggle, scrumptious, wacky, beatnik, sockdologer, ixnay, scram, payola, teenybopper, pizzaz, grandiferous.*

Some slang words are formed from other words by abbreviation or by adding new endings to change the part of speech: *legit, phony, VIP, psych out, snafu, C-note, groovy, nervy, mod.*

Sometimes words in acceptable use are given extended meanings: *smack, buck, chicken, mainline, bean, dish, sack, grease, tough, snow, cat, acid, trip.*

Some slang is formed by compounding or bringing together two or more words: *egghead, hepcat, stash* (store and cache), *sweedle,* (swindle and wheedle), *go-go girl, fly-boy.* The word *slanguage* used in the title of this chapter is a combination of "slang" and "language."

Slang often consists of one or more coined words combined with one or more standard terms: *blow one's top, shoot the bull, live it up, get in orbit, off one's rocker, jam session, shoot the works.*

Here is a list of expressions that illustrate the various methods by which slang is formed. If you don't recognize every item (or all of the slang terms just mentioned) remember that your inability to do so makes two good reasons why you should not overuse slang in speaking: it is not always understandable; it is often short-lived.

SLANG WORDS AND EXPRESSIONS

all-fired
applesauce
attaboy (attagirl)
babe
back number
baloney
bamboozle
barf
barge in
bats
battle-ax
beanery
beat one's brains out
beef
bench warmer
big shot
bigwig
bitch up
blind date
bloke
blow your stack
bollix (or bollicks)
booboo
bottoms up
brass hat
bread (money)
break it up
broad
bushed
buzz off
cabbage
carry the torch
chick
chips are down
chump
clip joints

coffee and cakes
conk (conk out)
cool it
cop a plea
cop out
cornball
crackpot
cramp one's style
cut the mustard
dago red
dame
dark horse
deadbeat
dead duck
dimwit
dish of tea
double dome
draw a blank
elbow grease
eyewash
fair-haired boy (girl)
fall for
far out
feds
fishy
flack
flapdoodle
flatfoot
flesh-peddler
flivver
floozy
flossy
folding money
fork over
four flusher
fuzz

gatecrasher	jack
geezer	jeez
get lost	jerk
get one's goat	jinx
get with it	jughead
girlie	kangaroo court
gismo (gizmo)	keep cool
gogetter	kibosh
goldbrick	kick around
gold digger	kickback
goner	kick in
goo	kick the bucket
gooey	kid
goof off (up)	know from nothing
gook	lay an egg
goon	lead balloon
goose egg	lettuce
gravy train	like crazy
grub	long green
gung ho	long time no see
gunk	lulu
guts	lummox
guy	made the scene
gyp joint	meat and potatoes
hair of the dog	meathead
halfbaked	moniker
halfcocked	monkey on one's back
hard sell	mooch
heavy	moola
hick	moxie
high-hat	muscle in
high-tail	natch
hogwash	nix
hokum	nudnik
hooey	nut
horse's mouth	nut house
hot air	nuts
hunkydory	nutty

okay
on the ball
on the beam
on the level
on the loose
on the make
on the wagon
oodles
oomph
pad
pappy
pantywaist
party pooper
peach
peachy keen
phiz
phony
piker
pip-squeak
poop
pork barrel
press the flesh
pusher
put up or shut up
ratfink
rat race
raunchy
razz
razzberry
razzledazzle
razzmatazz
rhubarb
ritzy
rub elbows with
sad sack
salad days
sawbuck
scads

schmaltz
screw
screwball
screw loose
screw out of
screwy
shakes
shebang
shell out
shenanigans
shiv
shove it
shyster
simoleon
sitting pretty
slaphappy
smart money
snow job
soft sell
soul kiss
sound off
split the scene
spot, on the
stool pigeon
sucker
sure thing
swing
threads
tizzy
turkey
turn off
turn on
twerp
upchuck
weirdie
weirdo
whammy
wheelerdealer

whodunit

wisenheimer

wise guy

yak (yack, yuk)

wise up

As you talk your way to a better job, don't tighten up and try to avoid slang altogether. It can't be done. It shouldn't be done, either, because some people who hear you won't object to slang and because giving up slang entirely might make your talk seem stiff and artificial. Talk slang in moderation. Use it only when it more clearly and more forcefully expresses what you have in mind than standard expressions would. Such occasions won't occur as often as you may think.

By being so long in the lowest form I gained an immense advantage over the cleverer boys. . . . I got into my bones the essential structure of the ordinary English sentence—which is a noble thing.

Winston Churchill

CHAPTER 15

Don't Be a Rubber Stamp

Many of the people we talk with bore us because they never seem to have anything new to say. Day after day, they use the same old words to express the same old thoughts. We exchange words with such persons because we see and work with them, but our conversations give us no pleasure, no lift, and little, if any, new information.

Is it possible that others feel the same way about you? Could it be that some persons think they know in advance what you're going to say and even the words and phrases you're going to use?

It's true that nearly everyone has formed the habit of speaking in molds of thought and expression, frequently repeated. Certain ways of saying things have become fixed in our minds, so fixed that we use them without real thought and without any genuine effort to express ourselves differently.

Avoiding as many dead and lifeless expressions in speech as possible is an excellent way to impress others with one's ability to communicate freshly and interestingly. Not everyone in a position to help you get ahead will be struck with your desire to avoid triteness, but somewhere along the line someone will be.

Triteness, sometimes referred to as *hackneyed language*, or *clichés*, applies to all words and expressions that are worn out from overuse. You will recognize most of the trite expressions listed later in this chapter because you have heard and used them again and again. And yet you should keep in mind that certain ways of saying things which seem fresh and original to you may be clichés to those who have read and listened more than you have.

The words *triteness, hackneyed language,* and *cliché* have origins that explain their meaning: *triteness* comes from the Latin word *tritus*, the past participle of a verb meaning "to rub, to wear out." *Hackneyed* is derived from the idea of a horse, or carriage (hackney coach), let out for hire, devoted to common use, and therefore exhausted in service. *Cliché* comes from the French word *clicher*, meaning "to stereotype," "to cast from a mold."

Trite expressions resemble slang in that both are stereotyped manners of thought and expression. Clichés may be stampings from common speech, outworn phrases, or overworked quotations. Usually they express good ideas (or ideas considered good) and are expressed in effective phrasing. (If they were not sensible and appealing, they would never have been used so much as to become stale.) The problem with clichés is not that they are inexpressive but that they have been overused and misused to the point of weariness and ineffectiveness.

COMMONLY USED TRITE EXPRESSIONS

The following examples of hackneyed language will alert you to your use and overuse of them. The suggestion here is not that you never use any of them but that you use them only after you have failed to think of a fresher or newer way to express what you have in mind. Like slang, clichés provide an excuse to avoid searching for the exact and specific wording everyone should seek.

absence makes the heart grow
   fonder
accidents will happen
acid test
add insult to injury
after one's own heart
age before beauty

alive and kicking
all in a lifetime
all in all
all in the day's work
all that glitters is not gold
all things being equal
all things considered

all wool and a yard wide
all work and no play
any port in a storm
apple of one's eye
apple-pie order
armed to the teeth
as luck would have it
as the crow flies
at loose ends
at one fell swoop
back the wrong horse
bark up the wrong tree
bated breath
battle of life
beard the lion in his den
beat a hasty retreat
beat about the bush
bee in one's bonnet
behind the scenes
benefit of the doubt
best foot forward
best-laid plans of mice and men
better half (one's)
better late than never
better to have loved and lost
between the devil and the deep
    blue sea
beyond the pale
bitter end
blind with rage
blood is thicker than water
bloody but unbowed
blow off steam
blow one's horn
blue blood
blushing bride
blush of shame
bolt from the blue

born with a silver spoon
bosom of the family
bottomless pit
brave as a lion
brawny arms
break the ice
breathe a sigh of relief
bred in the bone
bright and early
bright future
bright young countenance
bring home the bacon
bring home to
briny deep
brown as a berry
brute force
budding genius
bundle of nerves
busy as a bee (beaver)
butterflies in (my) stomach
by and large
by leaps and bounds
caught red-handed
change of heart
checkered career
cheer to the echo
cherchez la femme
cherished belief
chip off the old block
clear as mud
cloud nine
cock and bull story
cold as ice
cold feet
cold sweat
cool as a cucumber
come to grief
common, or garden, variety

comparisons are odious

conspicuous by his (her) absence

cradle of the deep

crocodile tears

crow to pick

crown of glory

cut a long story short

cut off one's nose to spite one's face

cynosure of all eyes

dainty repast

damn with faint praise

dead certainty

dead giveaway

dead of night

deaf as a post

deliver the goods

depths of despair

die is cast

die the death

distance lends enchantment

dog days

dog in the manger

doomed to disappointment

down my alley

down to the last detail

downy couch

draw in one's horns

draw the line

dreamy expression

drown one's sorrows

drunk as a skunk

duck (fish) out of water

dull thud

dust and ashes

dust to dust

ear to the ground

eat, drink, and be merry

eat humble pie

eat one's hat

epoch-making

eternal triangle (the)

et tu, Brute

every inch a king

exception proves the rule

eye for an eye

eyes like stars

eyes of the world

face the music

facts of life

fair sex

fall on deaf ears

far cry

far from the madding crowd

fast and loose

fat as a pig

fate worse than death

fat's in the fire

favor with a selection

fearfully and wonderfully made

feather in his (her) cap

feather one's nest

feel one's oats

feet of clay

festive board

few and far between

few well-chosen words

fight like a tiger

fight tooth and nail

fill the bill

filthy lucre

fine and dandy

first and foremost

fish out of water

flash in the pan

flat as a pancake
flesh and blood
fly in the ointment
fly off the handle
fond farewell
food for thought
(a) fool and his money
fool's paradise
fools rush in
for better or worse
foregone conclusion
free as the air
fresh as a daisy
friend in need
garden (common) variety
generous to a fault
gentle as a lamb
get more than one bargained
   for
get one's number
get one's teeth into
get the sack
get the upper hand
get up on the wrong side
gift of tongues
gild the lily
gilded youth
give hostages to fortune
give the devil his due
glass of fashion
God's country
goes without saying (it)
golden mean
golden opportunity
(a) good time was had by all
goose hangs high
grand and glorious
grain of salt

graphic account (description)
greatness thrust upon . . .
great open spaces
green as grass
green-eyed monster
green with envy
grim reaper
gross exaggeration
hail fellow well met
hale and hearty
half the battle
hand-to-mouth
hapless victim
happy as a lark
happy ever after
happy pair
hard row to hoe
haughty stare
haul over the coals
have a bone to pick
head over heels
heart of gold
heartless wretch
heart-to-heart talk
hew to the line
high and dry
high on the hog
hit the nail on the head
hold the fort
hot as a pistol
hour of need
hungry as a bear
idle rich, the
if the truth be told
in a nutshell
in on the ground floor
interesting to note
intestinal fortitude

in the last (final) analysis
in the long run
in the nick of time
irons in the fire
irony of fate
itching palm, an
it goes without saying
it stands to reason
jig is up
Job's comforter
join the happy throng
keep the pot boiling
know the ropes
land-office business
lap of luxury
last but not least
last straw
law-abiding citizen
law unto himself (herself)
lay down the law, to
lead a dog's life
lean and hungry look
lean over backward
leave in the lurch
leave much to be desired
leave no stone unturned
left-handed compliment
left in the lurch
let one's hair down
let the cat out of the bag
lick into shape
life of the party
like a newborn babe
limp as a rag
little did I think
live and learn
lock, stock, and barrel
long arm of the law

mad dash
make a clean breast of
make bricks without straw
make ends meet
make hay while the sun shines
make night hideous
make no bones
make the punishment fit the
    crime
make things hum
man in the street
mantle of snow
march of time
mark time
meets the eye
mend one's ways
method in his madness
milk of human kindness
mind your p's and q's
missing the boat
moment of victory
moot question
more dead than alive
more easily said than done
more than meets the eye
Mother Nature
much in evidence
naked truth
necessary evil
needle in a haystack
needs no introduction
never a dull moment
new lease on life
nipped in the bud
not a shadow of doubt
not to be sneezed at
not worth a continental
number is up

of a high order
of the first water
Old Sol
on bended knee
on the ball (stick)
open and shut
open secret
opportunity knocks but . . .
other things being equal
out of sight, out of mind
over a barrel
over and done with
ox in the ditch
parting of the ways
pay the piper (fiddler)
penny for your thoughts
pick and choose
pillar of society
place in the sun
play fast and loose
play it by ear
play second fiddle
play up to
play with fire
point with pride
poor but honest
praise to the skies
pretty as a picture
pretty kettle of fish
pretty penny
proud parents
psychological moment
pull one's leg
pull the wool over . . .
pull up stakes
pure and simple
put a bug (flea) in one's ear
put all one's eggs in one basket

put on the dog
put one's best foot forward
rack one's brains
raining cats and dogs
read between the lines
read the riot act
reckon without one's host
red as a beet
red-letter day
rendered a selection
rest in peace
ring true
risk life and limb
rub the wrong way
rule the roost
sad to relate
sadder but wiser
salt of the earth
save for a rainy day
scared to death
seal one's fate
seamy side of life
seething mass
self-made man
sell like hot cakes
set one's cap for
set one's heart on
set up shop
seventh heaven
shake in one's shoes
shoot one's bolt
shuffle off this mortal coil
sick and tired
sight for sore eyes
sight to behold
silver lining
sing like a bird
sleep the sleep of the just

smell a rat
sow wild oats
spend money like water
start the ball rolling
steal one's thunder
stick in the craw
stranger than fiction
strong as an ox
stubborn as a mule
stuff and nonsense
stuffed shirt
survival of the fittest
take it easy
take the bull by the horns
tell tales out of school
tender mercies
tenterhooks, be on
terra firma
that is to say
through thick and thin
throw in the sponge
throw the book at
time and time again
time hangs heavy

time stood still
tired as a dog
tit for tat
too funny for words
too many irons in the fire
touch and go
truth to tell
turn over a new leaf
up in arms
vale of tears
view with alarm
wash one's hands of
wee small hours
well-earned rest
wet to the skin
wheels within wheels
where ignorance is bliss
wide open spaces
without further ado
wolf in sheep's clothing
words fail me
you can say that again
young man's fancy
your guess is as good as mine

FILLERS AND CONVERSATIONAL TAGS

In everyday speech, anyone is likely to use worn out phrases, weary words, and tired expressions. But another similar problem exists.

As we talk, most of us tend to throw into our remarks large numbers of tags and fillers that add little or nothing to what we're saying. For instance, if we need time to think what we're going to say next, we will pause and say "uh" or "ah" or "well." When we can't think of anything else to add, we end a statement with "and all like that" or "and everything." When we want to keep on talking but have nothing particular in mind, we might say "and," prolonging the sound of the word in hopes that our listener will let us keep going.

Each of the following fillers can successfully be used in talking, but the talk you hear (and perhaps make) is overloaded with them. Each of them is trite, overworked, and wordy. Avoid using as many of them as often as you can because they add only words to what you say and little or no meaning at all.

actually	in so many words
ah	interestingly enough
and all	know what I mean?
and all like that	like
and everything	on balance
anyway	on the average
as a matter of fact	say
by and large	so
by the same token	still and all
curiously enough	strangely enough
first of all	strictly speaking
first off	that is to say
frankly	uh
honestly	well
in other words	you know

The words and expressions listed in this chapter are flat, stale, and unnecessary—descriptions that you do not want applied to you as you talk your way to a better job.

The greatest thing a human soul ever does in this world is to see something and tell what it saw in a plain way. Hundreds of people can talk for one who can think.

John Ruskin

CHAPTER 16

Get Rid of Deadwood

Nearly everyone—perhaps you and I included—talks more than is necessary. In doing so, we use more words than needed. In rapid-fire talk, in the give-and-take of conversation, we are likely to repeat ourselves and to use words that are meaningless or unneeded. (When writing, we have a chance to go over our work and remove the excess.) Effective speech is economical, but using enough words to cover the subject and not too many is a standard of perfection, unattainable by most of us. But if we can grasp and keep in mind a few suggestions, our speech will become more concise and consequently more interesting and appealing. When talk becomes more and more interesting, the pay envelope of the person using it has a chance to fatten.

Conciseness, or brevity, alone does not guarantee effective speaking, but it is impossible for anyone to speak forcefully, clearly, and entertainingly when using several words where one would be sufficient. Look at the Golden Rule: it contains only eleven words. The Ten Commandments are given in seventy-five words. Lincoln's Gettysburg Address consists of only two hundred and sixty-seven words.

In trying to make your speech leaner and cleaner, consider these suggestions:

1. Don't use several words where one or two will serve.
2. Avoid overuse of the expressions "there is" and "there are."

3. Avoid adding words to an already-expressed idea.
4. Reduce predication.
5. Omit unnecessary details .
6. Watch out for gobbledygook.

These suggestions overlap somewhat, but each deserves careful attention. Don't skip over them lightly. Someone in authority over you may already be annoyed by your constant output of words, words, words.

1. Using several words where one or two would do.

A speaker was once asked whether certain rules should be observed. Instead of replying yes, he remarked, "The implementation of sanctions will inevitably eventuate in repercussions." A foreman suggested that an assistant give instructions to workers "very precisely and carefully." He might better have said "Give precise instructions." "Any typist who is qualified can become a member of the secretarial staff" may be shortened to "Any qualified typist can become a secretary." "I was waiting for her telephone call until I became frantic" can be shortened to "I was waiting frantically for her telephone call."

2. Avoid "there is" and "there are" constructions.

Usually "there" beginnings contain superfluous words, adding nothing. The words "there are" can be removed from the following sentence with no loss in meaning or force: "In this building there are five elevators awaiting inspection." Better: "In this building five elevators await inspection."

3. Don't add words to an idea already expressed.

When meaning is expressed or implied in a particular word or phrase, repeating the idea in additional words adds nothing but verbiage. Common examples of this fault are using *again* or *back* with verbs beginning *re*(repeat again, return back); using *more* and *most* with adjectives and adverbs ending in *er* and *est* (more slower, most quickest); *more* or *most* with such absolute-meaning adjectives as *unique, round, square,* and *equal.*

4. Reduce predication.

Reducing predication means decreasing the number of words used to make a statement. Consider these suggestions:

1. Combine two short sentences into one.
   FROM: He was a mechanic in a repair shop. He special-
   ized in fuel adjustment.
   TO: He was a garage mechanic, specializing in fuel
   adjustment.
2. Reduce a compound or complex sentence to a simple sentence.
   FROM: Greta Garbo was for many years an excellent
   actress, and everyone admired her talent.
   Everyone admired the talent of Greta Garbo,
   who was for many years an excellent actress.
   TO: Everyone admired the talent of Greta Garbo, for
   years an excellent actress.
3. Reduce a clause to a phrase.
   FROM: a haze that resembled the color of smoke
   TO: a haze the color of smoke
4. Reduce a phrase to a single word.
   FROM: a haze the color of smoke
   TO: a smoke-colored haze
5. Reduce two or more words to one.
   FROM: a foreman in the Department of Shipping
   TO: a shipping foreman
   FROM: are going to attend
   TO: will attend

5. Leave out unnecessary details.

The needless repetition of an idea without providing additional force or clearness is called *tautology*. This flaw is obvious
in the following sentence: This entirely new and novel innova-
tion in our program will delight our TV-viewing audience; it has
just been introduced for the first time and will cause pleasure to
many people who will be watching.

FAULTY:	Jill was anxious for Rick to succeed and eager that he do so.
	In all necessary essentials the work is completed and finished.
IMPROVED:	Jill was eager for Rick to succeed.
	In all essentials the work is completed.
WORDY:	Last winter the squash tournament was won by Bill Blandard with a racquet he had purchased two months before from a friend of his who had bought a new one made of catgut and who sold Bill his old one for $8.50.
IMPROVED:	Last winter the squash tournament was won by Bill Blandard with a racquet he had bought from a friend for $8.50.
STILL BETTER:	Last winter Bill Blandard won the squash tournament with a second-hand racquet.

6. Avoid using gobbledygook.

Gobbledygook is wordy, inflated, obscure, and often unintelligible verbiage. The term was coined by a former United States congressman, grown weary of involved government reports, who possibly had in mind the throaty sounds uttered by a male turkey.

The term *gobbledygook* is often applied to governmental and bureaucratic announcements which have been called "masterpieces of complexity." For example, note this pompous and complex sentence from a recent governmental bureau pamphlet: "Endemic insect populations cause little-realized amounts of damage to forage and timber." This stuffy sentence probably means: "Native insects do more damage to trees and grass than we realize." In another pronouncement from a Washington bureau, "the chance of war" was referred to, in gobbledygook, as "in the regrettable eventuality of a failure of the deterrence policy."

The use of gobbledygook is not confined to bureaucratic circles, either within or without national and state governments.

But pompous and involved language is so prevalent in those areas that two further illustrations may be cited. A recent announcement about Junior Conservation Corps Camps reads as follows:

> Section 103 authorizes the Director of the Office of Economic Opportunity to:
>
> (a) enter into agreement with any Federal, State, or local agency or private organization for the establishment and operation, in rural and urban areas, of conservation camps and training centers, and for the provision of necessary facilities and services, including agreements with agencies charged with the responsibility of conserving, developing, and managing the public natural resources of the nation and with protecting the public recreational areas, whereby the Corps enrollees may be utilized by such agencies in carrying out, under the immediate supervision of such agencies, programs planned by such agencies to carry out such responsibilities.

What the writer presumably meant to say in plain English, not gobbledygook, is:

> Section 103 authorizes the OEO Director to:
>
> (a) make agreements with any government agency or private group to set up and operate JCC camps and training centers; and make agreements with conservation agencies to use and supervise Corps enrollees on projects these agencies have on public lands.

A plumber, an often-told story goes, wrote to inform an agency of the United States government that he had found hydrochloric acid good for cleaning out pipes. Some bureaucrat responded with this gobbledygook: "The efficiency of hydrochloric acid is indisputable, but the corrosive residue is imcompatible with metallic permanence." The plumber responded that he was glad the agency agreed. After several more gobbledygookish letters, an official finally wrote what he should have originally: "Don't use hydrochloric acid. It eats the inside out of pipes."

A recent commentator has suggested that the first duty of schools is to be so soft-minded that children no longer "flunk."

Instead, they "experience a temporary lack of success in the daily learning situation." And here is a quotation from a financial adviser concerning shares of stock: "Overall, the underlying pattern, notwithstanding periods of consolidation, remains suggestive of at least further selective improvement over the foreseeable future." Possibly the writer meant to say: "Selected stocks will increase in price." How would you phrase it?

If you become aware of gobbledygook and avoid using it at any time, you can have fun by turning good, direct English into wordy, jargonish utterances. Possibly realizing how absurd gobbledygook is will insure your never using it. Who, for instance, would prefer "Too great a number of culinary assistants may impair the flavor of the consommé" to "Too many cooks spoil the broth"? If you can, laugh at the gobbledygook artist who turned "Birds of a feather flock together" into "Feathered bipeds of similar plumage will live gregariously." Why not try your own hand at turning familiar sayings into gobbledygook? Rewrite the following sentences in plain, understandable language.

1. You should manufacture desiccated alfalfa during solarized incandescence.

2. The capital of the Papal States was not constructed during a diurnal revolution of the globe.

3. It has come to our attention that herbage, when observed in that section of enclosed ground being the property of an individual other than oneself, is ever of a more verdant hue.

4. Seeking a suitable place for the purpose of courting a state of dormant quiescence during the first part of the crepuscular period and forsaking said suitable place during the first part of the matinal period results in myriad benefits to *homo sapiens*, among which benefits may be noted a substantial increase in body soundness, monies, and sagacity.

5. Much of an organization's effectiveness depends upon the adequacy of the data and information with which its employees work. The multifarious overlapping planning units have produced fragmented data, oriented toward single uses of land, and as these data were used by employees organized into single use office groupings, the problem was exacerbated.

As a still further step toward rooting out wordiness, study this list of expressions, each of which can usually be shortened without loss of effectiveness or meaning:

REDUCE THESE	TO THESE
a certain length of time	a certain time
advance planning	planning
am (is, are) going to	shall, will
are (am) of the opinion	believe
as a result of	because
at the present time	now
at this point in time	now
because of the fact that	because
before long	soon
by the time	when
call us on the telephone	telephone us
destroyed by fire	burned
due to the fact that	due to, since
during the time that	while
for the amount of	for
hurry up	hurry
in accordance with	by
inasmuch as	since
in case	if
in connection with	with
in lieu of	instead
in order to	to
in regard to	about
insofar as	because, since, as
in the event that	if
in the month of May	in May
in this day and age	today
in view of the fact that	since
it has come to our attention that	(begin with the word following *that*)
it is interesting to note that	(begin with the word following *that*)
I would appreciate it if	please

made the recipient of	was given
on condition that	if
one of the purposes (reasons)	one purpose (reason)
pay a visit to	visit
prior to	before
provided that	if
the field of biology	biology
the length of 5 yards	5 yards (or 5 yards long)
under date of July 5	of July 5
with the exception of	except

MORE DEADWOOD

Carefully examine the following list of wordy expressions. How many of them appear regularly in your speech? Be honest. Isn't some "reducing diet" indicated?

absolutely essential
advance forward
around about that time
audible to the ear
back up
bisect in two
call up on the phone
choose up
Christmas Eve evening
combine together
complete monopoly
completely unanimous
connect up with
consensus of opinion
continue on
cooperate together
cover over
descend down
each and everyone
endorse on the back
entirely eliminated

extreme prime importance
few (many) in number
final end (outcome)
first beginnings
first originators
four-cornered square
from whence
important essentials
individual person
join together
long length
loquacious talker
many in number
meet up with
more angrier
more better
more older
more paramount
more perfect
more perpendicular
most unique

most unkindest

necessary essential

necessary need

old adage

personal friend

recur again

reduce down

repeat again

resume again

retreat backward

return back

revert back to

rise up

round in form

separate out

(a) short half-hour

small in size

sunset in the west

talented genius

this afternoon at 4 P.M.

this morning at 8 A.M.

visible to the eye

Brevity has been called the soul of wit. In this remark, "wit" means understanding, not humor. If you want the statements you make to be clear, cut out the unneeded words they probably contain. Using *no* unnecessary words is impossible for everyone, but getting rid of most of the useless, time-consuming expressions that dot speech is a major step forward, an important part of your campaign to talk your way to a better job.

Talking and eloquence are not the same: to speak and to speak well are two things. A fool may talk, but a wise man speaks.

Ben Jonson

CHAPTER 17

What's a Good Sentence? (1)

We think in terms of words, talk in sentences, and write in paragraphs. Such a statement is not entirely correct, but it is to the extent that the basic unit of speaking is the sentence. And just what *is* a sentence?

A fully satisfactory, no-nonsense definition is difficult to arrive at because sentences take many different forms. One definition is that a sentence consists of one or more words that provide a listener (or reader) with a complete idea. The definition you probably learned in grammar school is that a sentence is a group of words containing a subject and predicate and expressing a complete thought. (The difficulty with this definition is that it leaves up in the air what a subject and predicate are, that sentences don't always have expressed subjects and predicates, and that not all so-called sentences state complete thoughts.) As for written sentences, you might say a sentence is something that begins with a capital letter and ends with a period or question mark. In speaking, a sentence begins with the first word said and ends when a speaker lowers his voice for a stop or raises it for a question.

Whatever sentences are or should be, everyone talks in them. Just as the words we use are "good" or "bad," so are the sentences we speak. Just as standards exist for the choice and use of words, so do standards for sentences. Every sentence, spoken or written, should be *clear, correct,* and *effective.* These words may mean little. What's clear to one hearer may not be to another. What's correct may make little difference to a listener who understands what you're saying. An effective sentence can be anything you say that someone grasps and responds to.

Many learned books have been written about the sentence, the item you speak by the hundreds everyday. And why not? The simple sentence has been called the greatest invention of the human intellect—an achievement worth much discussion and writing.

TWO POINTS AND TWENTY ERRORS

The sentences you speak really are a part of you and reveal more of what you are and think than perhaps you realize. As you talk your way to a better and more rewarding job, keep these two points in mind: (1) the form, structure, and variety of spoken sentences are important but require less close inspection than those that are written; (2) the first and most effective step toward better sentences is getting rid of the obvious and glaring mistakes made in forming them.

This chapter and the next one focus on those major errors that creep easily, naturally, and frequently into the speech of nearly everyone, regardless of his or her education and background. (The topic is considered in two chapters rather than one because it is involved and somewhat detailed.) These two chapters are not a complete statement concerning what sentences should be at their best, but they are an effort to help you become aware of sentence ways that may be holding you back.

Not each of the twenty flaws discussed will be noticed by everyone who hears you. Some of them may rarely be noted by anyone at all, largely because talk is more relaxed and informal than most writing. And yet each of these flaws does reflect negatively upon you, whether noticed or not. Someone in authority, moreover, will surely catch you up on one or more of them at some time. Becoming aware of these sentence errors will help you to speak (and write) with ease and confidence and will increase your chances for greater recognition of your job performance.

If the names (labels) given these flaws bother you, ignore them and concentrate on the mistakes. Also, if the grammatical terms used in explanation seem difficult, ignore them, too. Concentrate on the faults themselves.

1. The accordion sentence

An accordion sentence is a group of words which, like an accordion, is first pulled out and then pressed together. In such a sentence, one group of words depends upon what comes before it. When we are talking rapidly and thoughtlessly, it's easy to let ideas overlap in sentences such as these:

> It was an inexpensive radio which had been made in Japan which once had cheap labor.

> These are the children who feed to the squirrels the nuts which they buy on the corner that is near the park.

The remedy is to break up such sentences into two or more separate statements.

2. The "and which" sentence

Effective sentence construction requires us never to use "and which" (or "but which" or "who which") unless we use a preceding "which," "but," or "who" clause. Here are examples:

> This is a beautiful tennis court, *and which* you will enjoy playing on with your friends.

> He showed much energy at first, *but which* soon vanished.

> He is a man of intelligence, *and who* is an industrious worker.

The simplest method of correcting these three sentences is to omit the conjunctions or to add a "who clause" or "which clause": "He is a man who is intelligent and who is an industrious worker." Such revision, however correct, is wordy and ineffective. The sentence may be rewritten: "The man is intelligent and industrious."

3. The choppy sentence

Try not to chop up the thought of one effective statement into a series of short, jerky sentences. Such a series is not only monotonous and childlike, it also gives emphasis to unimportant ideas that don't deserve emphasis. Notice how easy it is to place choppily expressed ideas in a longer, fully effective statement:

> He picked up the pocketbook. He saw that it contained a large sum of money. He naturally wanted to keep it.

> Better: When he picked up the pocketbook, he saw that it contained a large sum of money which, naturally, he wanted to keep.

> It was dark. She was afraid to enter the room. She called her brother. He did not hear her. This terrified her more than ever.

> Better: Because it was dark, she was afraid to enter the room. When she called her brother, he did not hear her, and thus she was more terrified than ever.

4. The wordy sentence

The best sentences are concise, never wordy. *Concise* means "brief," "condensed." In sentence structure it implies that much is said in few words. Good speaking and writing result from a wealth of ideas and economy in words, not the reverse—a scarcity of thought and a flood of words. Even well-constructed sentences can be improved by deleting non-essential or redundant words, using direct word patterns for roundabout ones, and economizing on modifiers.

Many words commonly used contribute little to the meaning or structure of sentences. Such "deadwood" expressions may be illustrated by the italicized words which follow:

> Redundant: *Despite the fact that* he had always thought his foreman *to be of the* blunt *type*, he finally realized *him to be a* kindly *man*.

> Concise: He had always thought his foreman blunt, but he finally realized he was kindly.

A sentence such as "My typing had the effect of making the boss regret the decision which had led him to hire me" can be shortened to "My typing made the boss regret hiring me"—a reduction from nineteen words to eight.

5. The double negative sentence

This construction consists of the use of two negative words in the same statement: He *couldn't* find his friend *nowhere*. The double negative appears in correct French and, indeed, was used repeatedly by Shakespeare and Chaucer and many other great writers in English. Actually, a double negative can intensify a negative sense, but it is considered a questionable form of expression.

Informal talk is filled with expressions such as "can't scarcely," "haven't scarcely," "can't hardly," "can't help but," and the like. Such informal phrases are generally acceptable. But sentences such as these are illiterate and never acceptable:

> I *didn't* get *no* food.
> We *didn't* see *nobody* there.
> *Nobody isn't* going to tell me *nothing*.

6. The double reference sentence

A sentence is not clear unless a hearer or reader can tell to what or whom its words refer. The sentences below don't make good sense until they're corrected. (If you don't understand about pronouns and antecedents and don't care to learn, skip the grammatical explanations and pay attention to the corrections.)

The antecedent of every pronoun must be clear and definite. Vague reference can be corrected by (1) repeating the antecedent; (2) using a synonym for the antecedent: (3) changing the construction of the sentence.

Vague: The manager told Del that *he* would vote in the next election.

He took the books from the boxes and placed *them* on the floor.

Better: The manager told Del that he intended to vote in the next election. (The double reference is corrected by changing the construction of the verb phrase.)

Clear, *but awkward*: The manager told George that he (the manager) would vote in the next election. (The

double reference is corrected by repeating the antecedent.)

Better: He took the books from the boxes and placed the vol-
umes on the floor. (The faulty reference is corrected
by using a synonym for the antecedent.)

He removed the books and placed the boxes on the
floor. (The faulty reference is corrected by changing
the construction of the sentence.)

7. The faulty comparison sentence

Comparison is the change in the form of an adjective or
adverb to show greater or smaller degrees of quantity, manner,
or quality. The three degrees of comparison are positive, comparative, and superlative. Several errors in comparison are not
only possible in sentence construction; they are all too frequent.

Use the comparative degree with two, the superlative with
more than two. In informal usage we hear such a statement as
"Navy's team is the *best*" when only two teams are being compared. Careful speakers would use *better* in such a sentence.

Bring me the *better* of those knives. (Two knives concerned.)

Bring me the *best* of those knives. (Three or more knives
concerned.)

Avoid including the subject compared if the subject is part of
the object with which it is compared.

Wrong: She is older than any girl in her group.
Correct: She is older than any *other* girl in her group.

In informal and colloquial English the superlative is sometimes used when no particular comparison is intended: "You
are *most* generous." Such a use of *most* is rare.

Faulty comparisons are also caused by leaving out necessary
words. Do not omit *as* or *than* in double comparison; do not
omit the standard of comparison or one term of the comparison.

Doubtful: I study my manual harder than Fred.
Improved: I study my manual harder than Fred does.

I study my manual harder than I study Fred.

Doubtful: He is as strong, if not stronger, than John.

Improved, *but awkward*: He is as strong *as*, if not stronger
than, John.

Preferable: He is as strong as John, if not stronger.

Doubtful: He is so weak.

Improved: He is so weak that he cannot do any work.

Doubtful: This is the best cake.

Improved: This *is* the best cake I have ever eaten.

8. The fragmentary sentence

An incomplete sentence in speaking is not nearly so serious a
flaw as one in writing. Each of us constantly makes remarks
that don't form complete sentences but that do make sense.
There's nothing wrong with talking like the following exchange,
although only the first sentence is "complete":

"Did you buy it?"
"Yes."
"How much?"
"Ten dollars."
"Too much."
"Maybe so."

Skilled writers occasionally use fragmentary sentences to
achieve some stylistic effect. Skilled speakers often use incomplete sentences because it's natural and not always incorrect to
do so. In speaking, however, it's not a bad idea to form into a
complete statement what comes after you drop your voice to
mark the end of a statement. Study the following examples,
omitting the grammatical comments if you wish:

I had no money for a trip to Europe. *When suddenly I was
left a fortune.* (Dependent clause.)

I labored hours every night. *Finally giving up all my efforts.*
(Participial phrase.)

The bank was destroyed by those who needed it most. *The
small depositors.* (Appositive phrase.)

Such fragmentary sentences may be corrected by rephrasing or by joining the dependent clause or phrase to a preceding or following whole sentence.

Revised: I had no money for a trip to Europe. Suddenly I was left a fortune.

I labored hours every night but finally gave up all my efforts.

The bank was destroyed by those who needed it most, the small depositors.

9. The fused sentence

In writing, it's a serious blunder to put two sentences together with no mark of punctuation between them. In speaking, however, the problem is not nearly so great. And yet you will "fuse" or "blend" two sentences if you don't drop your voice or make a brief pause after the first one. If you speak rapidly, running your words together, you will fuse statements and confuse listeners.

What follows applies to written sentences. If you will let the use of your voice substitute for the punctuation marks mentioned, you will easily understand what is meant by "fusing" sentences.

A sentence is a complete and independent statement and should always be followed by a full stop, that is, a terminal mark of punctuation.

Wrong: The automobile ran smoothly the train was rough.

The next day he departed for Atlanta this city is the capital of Georgia.

Judged by their grammatical form, each of those two "sentences" contains two independent statements. Each "sentence" may be written as two separate sentences or, if the writer feels that the statements are sufficiently related in thought, other punctuation may be used. The result might be a compound sentence with a semicolon separating the clauses and a terminal mark at the end:

Revised: The automobile ran smoothly. The train was rough.

The automobile ran smoothly; the train was rough.

The methods used to avoid the *fragmentary sentence* (which see) may be applied to many fused sentences. For example, you may subordinate one of the statements: The next day he departed for Atlanta, the capital of Georgia.

10. The implied reference sentence

A sentence can fail to make sense if a word which it should contain is omitted. This mistake occurs frequently in everyday talk, usually involving that part of speech called pronouns.

One of the most common forms of implied reference is the use of the pronouns *this, which, that*, etc., to refer to an entire preceding statement rather than to some word in that statement.

Vague: His brother is a dentist. *This* is the profession he intends to enter.

I like to travel in Switzerland. *They* are always pleasant to visitors.

I cannot answer your letter *which* makes me very sad.

Improved: His brother is a dentist. Dentistry is the profession he intends to enter.

I like to travel in Switzerland. The Swiss are always pleasant to visitors.

I cannot answer your letter, a fact which makes me very sad.

or

It makes me very sad to think that I cannot answer your letter.

Note: Faults in the reference of *this, which, that*, etc., may be corrected by (1) summing up the idea of the preceding statement in a noun which acts as the antecedent; (2) making the statements co-ordinate; (3) rephrasing the sentence.

CHAPTER 18

What's a Good Sentence? (2)

Before reading this chapter, briefly review the first seven paragraphs of Chapter 17. What follows is discussion of another ten flaws in sentence construction of which you should become aware.

11. The indefinite "it," "they," and "you" sentence

It, they, and *you* are vaguely and loosely used in much of our talking.

INDEFINITE "IT"

It, as a third person singular pronoun, neuter, should usually have an appropriate antecedent. When *it* is used impersonally (*it* seems, it is possible, *it* is raining, etc.), another *it* should not be used in the same sentence referring to a definite antecedent.

Dubious: In this picture *it* showed some of the dark side of rural life.

Better: This picture showed some of the dark side of rural life.

Dubious: In this magazine article *it* states that not all wars are victories for the victors.

Better: This magazine article states that not all wars are victories for the victors.

Dubious: Bar Harbor is a beautiful summer resort; we liked *it* and *it* is possible that we shall go there again.

Better: We liked Bar Harbor as a summer resort, and *it* is possible that we shall go there again.

Dubious: Our roof needs patching, and when *it* rains hard, *it* leaks badly.

Better: Our roof needs patching, and *it* leaks badly in heavy rain.

INDEFINITE "THEY"

They, their, theirs, them, as plural forms of the third person personal pronoun, should have definite antecedents: plural nouns or pronouns. Otherwise, these pronouns should not be used.

Dubious: *They* have good roads in Texas.

Better: Texas has good roads.

Dubious: *They* say that Mexico is becoming very popular among tourists.

Better: Many people are saying that Mexico is becoming popular among tourists.

Dubious: We do our shopping in Chicago, for we like *their* large department stores.

Better: We do our shopping in Chicago, for we like that city's large department stores.

INDEFINITE "YOU"

In informal and colloquial speaking and writing, an expression such as "You can see the importance of money" is permissible, even though *you* may refer to no particular person or group. In general, however, when using *you*, be sure that you mean the person or persons whom you are addressing. For example, the following is inappropriate in speaking to adults: "When you become a Boy Scout, *you* learn many useful things." If you wish to refer to a number of people in general and to no one in particular, use indefinite pronouns like *one, anyone, a person*.

Dubious: In meetings *you* should do more speaking.

Preferable: In meetings the participants should do more speaking.

When a youngster becomes a Boy Scout, he learns many useful things.

12. The "is when," "is where," and "is because" sentence

These terms are frequently misused, especially in giving definitions. Grammatically, the fault may be described as using an adverbial clause in place of the noun phrase or clause which is called for. "A subway *is where* you ride under the ground" can be improved to "A subway *is* (or *involves*) an electric railroad beneath the surface of the streets." "Walking *is when* you move about on foot" can be improved to "Walking *is* the *act* of (or *consists of*) moving about on foot."

No one would argue for such a stentence as "A good time *is when* you have plenty of money and an attractive date." Nevertheless, "the reason is because" occurs occasionally. Standard usage insists upon "the reason is that."

13. The "misplaced modifier" sentence

Some of the sentences you say may not be clear to others because of the way you arrange words. Words in an English sentence have meaning largely because of their position. That is, they have one meaning in one position, another meaning in another position, and little or no meaning in still another position. "My *first* foreman's name was Bill" has a meaning different from "My foreman's *first* name was Bill." Again, changing the position of only one word results in ideas that are quite unalike: I was invited to a dance *tonight*. I was *tonight* invited to a dance.

Try to keep related words together so that your readers may see the connection you have in mind; try to place every modifier so that logically and naturally it is associated with the word or phrase it modifies.

In some of the sentences you speak, you may use what is called a "squinting modifier." A modifier "squints" when it "looks both ways" and may refer to either of two parts of a sentence. Consider this sentence: The person who can do this *well* deserves praise.

Well may modify either *can do* or *deserves*. One way to clear up the confusion is to add *certainly* after *well*. Now the adverb *well* modifies *can do*, and the adverb *certainly* applies to *deserves*.

Take another example: The repairman who does his work quietly *from the point of view of the housewife* is worthy of praise. The "squinting" italicized phrases should appear at the beginning or end of the sentence, which will still be wordy and awkward but at least understandable.

Still another way to confuse your listeners is to misplace such words as "only," "even," "hardly," "scarcely," and "not." Words such as these are usually associated with the word or phrase immediately following or preceding. In this sentence, *He hardly has enough strength for the work, hardly* may be thought to modify *has*; it shoud logically modify the adjective *enough*. To remove any possible doubt, write: He has *hardly* enough strength for the work.

Here is a sentence containing eleven words: *Only the foreman told me to finish the job before noon.* In it the word *only* can appear in every position from one through eleven: The *only* foreman told me. . . . , the foreman *only* told me. . . . , the foreman told *only me*. . . . , and so on. The position of *only* will provide eleven somewhat different meanings for the sentence.

Unless we are careful, we are likely to say some sentences that have a "dangling" part. Any misplaced word, phrase, or clause dangles in the sense that it hangs loosely within a sentence. The word another word or group of words is intended to modify should never be taken for granted; it should be expressed and it should be placed so that your hearers can easily make the intended association. Sentences containing dangling phrases may be corrected in three ways: (1) by expanding the phrase to a clause; (2) by supplying the noun or pronoun that the dangling phrase *should* modify; (3) by placing the construction so near the supplied word that no confusion is possible.

Incorrect: *Walking down the aisle*, the curtain rose. (Participial phrase)

                To play tennis well, a good racquet is needed. (Infinitive phrase)

                By exercising everyday, your health will improve. (Gerund phrase)

Correct: While we were walking down the aisle, the curtain rose.

                Walking down the aisle, John saw the curtain rise.

                We, walking down the aisle, saw the curtain rise. (This revision is no great improvement because it widely separates subject and verb.)

The two other incorrect sentences given may also, be improved by one of the three methods suggested. Most of us don't mind making an error, but we do dislike being thought incoherent or ludicrous, both of which these sentences definitely are.

When a verbal phrase is used to denote a general action rather than a specific one, it is *not* considered a dangling modifier: *Considering everything*, his suggestion was reasonable.

The position of modifiers also causes trouble in sentences that have something omitted, as many of the sentences we speak do. Look at these examples:

Incorrect: *When 19 years old*, my grandfather died.
               While working last night, the lights went out.
               Before thoroughly warmed up, you should not race a motor.

To correct such confused sentences, insert in the dangling clause the needed subject and verb, or change the subject (or subject and verb) in the main clause.

     When I was 19 years old, my grandfather died.

     When 19 years old, I grieved because my grandfather had died.

     While I was working last night, the lights went out.

Before it is thoroughly warmed up, you should not race a motor.

You should thoroughly warm up a motor before you race it.

14. The rambling sentence

When we talk, our thoughts often wander and we find it hard to stick to the subject we're discussing. When this happens, we ramble, we include details that don't belong, we "jump the track" of our thought. Such talk is hard to follow and makes our hearers wonder if we know what we're talking about. Every sentence you speak should have unity, a singleness of purpose. It should stick to one thought or to closely related thoughts.

Sentence unity does not mean that only one object or idea should be mentioned or that the sentence must be short. A unified sentence may refer to several people, places, objects, or ideas, and may be lengthy. For example, this is a unified sentence: "Although the weather had turned warmer during the night, nevertheless Jim and I decided to pack our provisions and sharpen our skates in the hope that our guide would decide the ice was still safe for skating." The sentence is long and refers to several things and people; but it is unified because it has a singleness, a oneness, of purpose. But a sentence could be one-fourth as long as this and refer to only one person, and yet violate the principle of unity: "Joe was a good mechanic, being the possessor of a new hat."

(1) Introducing too many details and (2) combining unrelated ideas violate sentence unity, essential to clear speaking. Avoid rambling sentences which introduce too many details.

Wrong: They offered to meet our party at Moose Junction, a little town in Minnesota which has only five hundred inhabitants, but which contains two general stores, three churches, and, since 1933, several saloons and a distillery owned by a wealthy man named Parks.

Revised: They offered to meet our party at Moose Junction, a little town in Minnesota which has only five hundred inhabitants, two general stores, and three churches. Since 1933, it has maintained several saloons and a distillery. The latter is owned by a wealthy man named Parks.

Avoid placing unrelated ideas in the same sentence.

Wrong: The grass was cut short, and she had bought the seed from Mrs. Thomas.

The woman wore a white dress, and she had a good time at the reception.

Sometimes you can attain unity by making one idea subordinate to the other in the sentence, but ideas so unrelated as those immediately above should be placed *in separate sentences*.

I decided to go skating that afternoon, using some skates that I had bought for a low price earlier in the day.

The town in which he formerly lived was small, it having a population of only one thousand, more than half of whom worked in the Smith and Brown Mattress Factory, Inc.

These two sentences are so wordy that whole ideas might be deleted. From the first, omit mention of price: "I decided to go skating that afternoon, using some skates that I had bought earlier in the day." If the matter of price is important, say it in another sentence. The second sentence contains two distinct ideas which may be placed in separate sentences or which may be combined and shortened: "He formerly lived in a town of only one thousand, more than. . . ."

15. The "reason is because" sentence

In standard English, the construction beginning "The reason is . . ." is followed by a noun or a noun clause usually introduced by *that*. Yet we often hear such a sentence as "I couldn't go; the *reason was because* I had to work." In spite of its form, the construction introduced by "reason was . . ." is a noun clause rather than an adverbial one. But such a use should appear only in informal speech. Standard usage requires "I couldn't go; the reason *was that* I had to work."

16. The "seesaw" sentence

Such a sentence takes its name from the familiar playground device. A group of such sentences moves up and down and quickly becomes monotonous. Sentences such as the following appear all too often in talk:

> We thought of going to a movie or a bowling alley, but we didn't have enough money. Next we decided to take a walk, but it began to rain. We bought some soft drinks and we went to Jack's house to watch TV. Soon Jack started snoring, and the rest of us became restless and bored.

17. The "shifty" sentence

A shifty sentence is not always "tricky," but it is one that can shift its parts in any of several ways. Such shifts may occur in (a) structure; (b) class or person of pronouns: (3) figures of speech; (d) number; (e) subject and voice; (f) tense.

(a) *Shift in sentence structure.* Shifting from one form to another may cause confusion. An adjective should be paralleled by another adjective, active or passive voice should remain consistent within a sentence, etc. Shifted constructions in sentences defeat clarity and are a sign of carelessness or ignorance. You should not begin a sentence with one construction and then shift, for no good reason, to another.

(b) *Shifts in class or person of pronouns.* This error violates the general rule that pronouns and antecedents must agree in person. The most common occurrence of this fault is shifting from the third person to the second:

> If *one* tries hard enough, *you* will inevitably succeed. (*One* is an indefinite pronoun in the third person; *you* is a personal pronoun, second person.) The sentence should read "If *you* try hard enough, *you*. . . ." or "If *one* tries hard enough, *he*. . . ."

(c) *Shifts in figures of speech.* A figure of speech is an expression using words in an unusual or nonliteral sense to give freshness or beauty to style. You should not shift suddenly from figurative language to literal speech, or vice versa. You should sustain one figure of speech and not shift to another. Through shifting, we get such a "mixed" figure as this:

When Anne lost her job, she got into a rut and felt all at sea.

(d) *Shifts in number.* A common error in the use of number is a shift from plural to singular, or singular to plural, or failure to make pronouns and antecedents agree in number.

If *men* really try *their* best *he is* bound to succeed. (Change *he* to *they* and *is* to *are.*

A small child can be a great joy, but *they require* much care. (Change *they* to *he* or *she*; *require* to *requires.*

(e) *Shifts in subject and voice.* Is the subject of a given sentence *acting* (active voice) or *being acted upon* (passive voice)? Sentences are always more effective if one voice is consistently used throughout a passage.

The furnace burns little coal, and at the same time Jim says it is easily cleaned. (Jim says the furnace. . . .)

As you look across the street, tall trees can be seen. (. . . street, you can see . . .)

(f) *Shifts in tense.* Maintain one point of view in time unless there is excellent reason for changing. Do not change the tense from present to past or from past to present in narration.

Incorrect: George was walking slowly down the street when suddenly an automobile turned the corner. It dashes wildly down the avenue, careening and twisting as if its driver is crazy. George jumped behind a tree to protect himself. (Change *dashes* to *dashed, is* to *were.*)

18. The overused "so" sentence

Even though *so* is correctly used in many sentences, the chief objection to *so* is *overuse*. In constructions like those below, *so* can often be replaced by *therefore, since, thus, accordingly*, and the like.

Ineffective: The bridge was out on Route 8, *so* we had to make a long detour on Highway 20.

Improved: Since the bridge was out on Route 8, we had to make a long detour on Highway 20.

Sometimes *so* is misused when the speaker means *so that* or *in order that*:

Ineffective: Do people want the government to spend more money *so* they can pay higher taxes?

Improved: Do people want the government to spend more money *in order that* they can pay higher taxes?

19. The "telegraphic" sentence

Speaking and writing can be understood even when important words are omitted. (Otherwise, many important telegrams and cables would be misinterpreted.) The following, however, is not good style in conversation; talk should be direct and brief but not curt and clipped: "Letter received. Leaving tomorrow noon. Reserve room Barrett Hotel. Regards."

20. The "vague reference" sentence

In clear talk, every pronoun (*especially that, these, those, it*) should refer clearly to its antecedent or should be made clear by some other statement in the sentence.

Faulty: His attitude gave me *that* sinking feeling.

Better: His attitude gave me a sinking feeling

or

His attitude depressed me.

Faulty: In this magazine article *it* states that war is not inevitable.

Better: This magazine article states that, etc.

Faulty: *They* say that Alaska is a potentially wealthy state.

Better: It is said that Alaska is, etc.

Faulty: This book is so written that the reader may study any one section and so that *it* may be studied as a unit.

Better: This book is so written that the reader may study any one section or this section may be studied as a unit.

Faulty: When a salesman hands over an article to a customer, *he* is not always certain of its worth.

Better: A salesman *is* not always certain of the worth of an article when, etc.

Be precise in using such reference words as *former, latter, first, second, third, last;* make certain your hearer can understand exactly the point you have in mind.

Take care with the sentences you speak. They are an index to the way your mind works.

After you have made certain that you understand the twenty flaws presented in Chapters 17 and 18, test yourself by finding the mistakes in the following sentences and suggesting a correction for each.

A

1. Because the handwriting was illegible. The order was not filled.
2. Last summer the restaurant was closed for repairs to all customers.
3. After looking everywhere, the gloves were found under the table.
4. With bad weather, our company picnic will be cancelled, with lack of sufficient interest.
5. This is a beautiful room, and which we enjoy using it often.
6. Will Rogers once said that if you encourage people to talk about themselves that you will hear nothing but good.
7. Bravery is when someone shows grace under pressure.

8. They say that falling in love is a wonderful experience.
9. The scarecrow did not frighten the birds it attracted them in flocks.
10. In the article it explained why cars soon wear out without proper care.

B

1. If you worked hard enough, one will be sure to get ahead.
2. They say that the candidate is only a slick politician.
3. We haven't got but just enough stock on hand to fill the order.
4. Dick began to feel sleepy, stretched out on the floor, and so he took a nap.
5. When Clyde got his first paycheck it almost seemed like a million dollars.
6. Our foreman has, believe it or not, been here for thirty years.
7. John is studying to be an accountant. This is a profession he admires.
8. The reason Deirdre was late this morning is because her alarm clock failed to go off.
9. I only have three dollars to last until payday.
10. She is a harder worker than any girl in her office.

CHAPTER 19

Building and Using a Vocabulary

Not being able to think of the right words to express what we want to say is a frustrating, baffling experience that happens to most of us every day. Lack of mastery of words prevents people from revealing their thoughts, impressions, and ideas and holds them back from the advancement they want and probably need.

Nearly everyone recognizes how important vocabulary (one's stock of words) is. If you are someone who doesn't, give thought to this statement by a scientific investigator:

An extensive knowledge of the exact meanings of English words accompanies outstanding success in this country more often than any other single characteristic which the Human Engineering Laboratory has been able to isolate and measure.

No one owns a fully satisfactory word supply, a condition most people are willing to concede. At one time or another, most persons make some sort of effort to acquire a better vocabulary. But the difficulty is that no easy methods exist for doing this. The simplest way to start, however, is by learning to use the words we already know. In part, this task involves "losing" from our vocabularies the unacceptable words and expressions discussed in previous chapters, especially 10–15.

Each of us has three vocabularies. First, there is our *active*, or *speaking*, vocabulary. This is our productive word stock, the words we use daily in speech. Second, there is our *writing* vocabulary. This also is active in that we use it in writing, even though it contains some words that we seldom use in speech. In addition to these two active, or productive, vocabularies, each of us has a *potential*, or *recognition*, vocabulary.

Using this potential vocabulary (the largest of the three), we can understand speakers and can read and understand books, magazines, and newspapers. But in our reading and listening we come across many words which we recognize and of which we have some understanding, but which we are unable to use in our own speaking and writing. Until we use such words, however—put them into circulation, that is—they are not really ours.

To get words from our potential into our active vocabularies requires systematic effort, but it is the logical way to begin vocabulary improvement. Words in a recognition vocabulary already have made some impression on our consciousness; they are already partly ours. Their values, although still vague to us, can be made exact and accurate. Furthermore, quite likely they are words that we want in our vocabularies. Probably we have come across them time and again. They are not unusual; they are words that have *use* value.

What follows is a test designed to prove that you *do* have a recognition vocabulary consisting of some words that you might wish to make active in everyday speech. Select in each series of this test the word or word group that is closest in meaning to the word italicized in the preceding phrase. You may not have full understanding of each of the 25 words involved, but you are certain to know some of them. If you know less than half of them, get busy with the suggestions that follow. And don't peek at the answers given on page 151 until you have really worked at the test:

1. *lucidity* of explanation   vagueness/wordiness/
                                        fertility/brevity/clearness

2. an ugly *scowl*   boat/look/nose/statement/
                                        skull

3. an *irrelevant* remark   pertinent/cute/irreverent/
                                        unrelated/brilliant

4. never *procrastinate*   forget/delay/hurry/
                                        prophesy//overeat

5. *exotic* perfumes — excellent/ordinary/sweet/ expensive/foreign

6. an *orthodox* belief — ordinary/mistaken/religious/ approved/pagan

7. to *obliterate* all traces — witness/destroy/investigate/ emphasize/ignore

8. an *incredulous* person — insincere/kind/inefficient/ unbelieving/skillful

9. to speak *monotonously* — tiresomely/alone/vigorously/ effectively/clearly

10. financial *solvency* — saving/transaction/debt/ soundness/contract

11. lost in a *maze* — amazement/marsh/ confusion/mirth/surprise

12. *spontaneous* applause — unpremeditated/forced/ insincere/loud/pleasing

13. a *synonymous* word — harsh/illiterate/difficult/easy/ similar

14. to *tantalize* a child — tease/please/titillate/adopt/ caress

15. to *assimilate* food — desire/need/buy/absorb/ reject

16. a *somnolent* atmosphere — sleepy/clear/warm/cloudy/ healthful

17. to *concoct* an alibi — destroy/prepare/ignore/ insinuate/concentrate on

18. a *potent* medicine — bitter/pleasant/patented/ powerful/expensive

19. a *rendezvous* in New York — friend/appointment/ apartment/show/night club

20. reached the *zenith* — horizon/rim/top/zero point/ goal

21. an unkind *allusion* — act/reference/insult/illusion/ admission

22. the *limpid* water — cold/muddy/clear/obscure/ purified

23. a *precarious* position — desirable/premeditated/peril- ous/elevated/misunder-

	stood
24. to be *arraigned* in court	invited/acquitted/accused/ presented/sentenced
25. all kinds of *vitality*	victuals/drink/people/ necessities/vigor

In trying to improve the quality of your stock of words and increase its size and range, three plans will be useful; (1) listening, (2) reading, and (3) studying a dictionary.

LISTENING

If you are like most people, you spend a lot of time with a radio or television set. Start *really* listening to what you hear— or, put another way—really pay attention to the sounds that strike your ears. Not every speaker you hear will use words acceptably, but in almost any broadcast or telecast you will encounter expressions that might be useful to you. Jot them down, look them up in a dictionary later, and—if they are words you could profitably use—try them out in your next conversation.

As you talk with others, notice what words are used. Some of them might be useful additions to your vocabulary. This is especially likely to be true when you talk with someone who is more experienced or better educated than you. (If you need help in learning to listen better, refer to Chapter 9.) When you hear a lecture or political talk, don't doze off. Have a notebook at hand and list words you hear that might increase your word supply. If you happen to be taking a class, listen to what your teacher and classmates say. You will learn a lot of words that might be useful.

READING

We have both to learn, and to learn how to use, words before they can become parts of our active vocabularies. Try reading the current issue of one of your favorite magazines, underlining all the words in it that you do not use often. Then try to give a working definition of each word and to use the word in a sentence. Even the most intelligent and well-educated readers usually discover when they put themselves through this test they have simply assumed that they know words which in fact they do not know. Probably a few of the words that you underlined will be useless, but most of them will be useful ones that you can add to your working vocabulary. Set out to master these words; move them from your potential to your active vocabulary.

If in reading you dislike to "break the chain of thought" by looking up words in a dictionary (although the very necessity for using a dictionary has already broken that chain), jot down unfamiliar words and look them up as soon as possible. Keeping a notebook nearby is a good idea. Be sure, after you have studied a new word, to use it in speaking until it is yours. Adding words to one's stock can be fascinating, but there must be a constant exercise of your will to study and use what you have gained.

Keep applying this exercise to much of what you read: other magazines, a daily newspaper, any book you pick up. Those who read a lot are not always effective speakers, but those who have read carefully have substantially increased their word stock, whether or not they realize it.

USING A DICTIONARY

Intelligent listening and thoughtful reading should lead straight to a good dictionary. Occasionally looking up a word in a dictionary will help very little. Sitting down in a burst of enthusiasm to learn scores of words is a waste of time. Trying to "swallow the dictionary" is stupid.

Aside from fixing in your mind the meanings and uses of specific words encountered, a dictionary can greatly increase your word supply if you will use it sensibly, regularly, and systematically. You can enlarge and strengthen your vocabulary in wholesale fashion if you will use a dictionary to learn about (1) synonyms and antonyms, (2) prefixes and suffixes, and (3) combining forms.

SYNONYMS AND ANTONYMS

Synonyms are words that in one or more of their definitions have the same or similar meanings as other words. *Antonyms* are pairs of words that have opposite, or negative, meanings.

Collecting lists of synonyms and distinguishing among their meanings is an effective, and often entertaining, way to enlarge your vocabulary. Most good dictionaries include listings and often brief discussions of hundreds of synonyms. When looking up a word, carefully study the treatment of those synonym entries that sometimes follow the definitions. If you do this, you may be able to choose a more exact and effective word for the occasion at hand and also add a useful word to your active vocabulary.

For example, after becoming aware of synonyms, will you necessarily have to write that the girl is *cute*, the game *thrilling*, the idea *interesting*, the dress *sexy* or *mod*, the play *exciting*? A study of synonyms for *old* might add to your vocabulary these, among other words: *immemorial, aged, ancient, aboriginal, decrepit, antique, hoary, elderly, patriarchal, venerable, passé, antiquated*, and *antediluvian*.

Similarly, studying antonyms will improve your understanding and also contribute to vocabulary growth. For example, seeking antonyms for *praise* may add to your vocabulary such words as *vilify, stigmatize, lampoon, abuse, censure, blame, deprecate, condemn, impugn, denigrate, disparage*, and *inveigh against*. Even such a simple word as *join* has numerous approximate opposites, among them *uncouple, separate, sunder, unyoke, cleave, disconnect*, and *dissever*.

PREFIXES AND SUFFIXES

Another method of adding to your vocabulary is to make a study of prefixes and suffixes.

A *prefix* is an element placed before a word or root to make another word of different function or meaning. (The prefix *pre* means *before: pre-American, premeditate, premature*.)

Knowing the meanings of some of the hundreds of prefixes in

words is helpful in getting at some sense of unfamiliar words. For instance, knowing that the prefix *ab-* means "from" or "away" will help you guess at the meanings of words such as *abduct* (to lead or carry away, to kidnap) and *absent* (to take or keep oneself away). Other words with the prefix *ab-*, all having some meaning of "away," "from," or "off," are these: *absolve, abort, abnormal, abjure, abolition, abdicate, abject, absolute, absorb*, and scores of others.

Following is a list of common prefixes, together with one or more approximate meanings and illustrative words:

a-	not	not, reverse of
ad-	to, against	amoral, anonymous
ambi-	around, both	adverse, adjective
ante-	before	ambiguous, ambidextrous
anti-	opposite	antedate, anteroom
audio-	hearing	antisocial, antiwar
auto-	self, same	audiovisual, audition
		autograph,
bene-	well, good	autobiography
bio-	life	beneficial, benefit
circum-	about, around	biography, biology
co-	complement of	circumstance, circumflex
col-	together	comaker, co-signer
com-	with, together	collateral, collection
de-	away, down, from	combine, compare
dis-	apart, not, away	demerit, degrade
ec- (ex-)	from, out of	disbar, disability
en- (em-)	in, on, into	eccentric, exhale
epi-	upon, before	enact, empower
ex-	out of, from	epigram, epilogue
extra-	beyond, without	exclaim, excommunicate
		extrajudicial,
hemi-	half	extrasensory
hyper-	beyond the	hemisphere, hemiplegia
	ordinary	hypercritical,
il-		hypersensitive
im-	not	illogical, illegitimate

inter-	opposed, negative among, between	immoral, imbalance interdepartmental, intercollegiate
intra-	within	intramural, intravenous
ir-	not, opposed	irreligious, irreducible
meta-	along with, among	metaphysics, metamorphism
mono-	one, alone	monochrome, monologue
neo-	new, recent	neophyte, neolithic
para-	beside	paragraph, parachute
per-	through, thoroughly	pervert, perfect
peri-	about, beyond	perimeter, perigee
poly-	many	polygon, polysyllable
post-	behind, after	postscript, postgraduate
pro-	for, forward	proclivity, proceed
pseudo-	false	pseudoclassic, pseudonym
re-	backward, again	revert, return
retro-	backward	retrogress, retroactive
semi-	half	semidetached, semicolon
super-	above, beyond	supernatural, supersensitive
syn-	together, with	synthesis, syndrome
tel- (tele-)	distant	telegraph, telecast
trans-	across, beyond	transcend, transmit
ultra-	beyond, in excess of	ultraviolet, ultrasonic
un-		unfair, unbend

A *suffix* is an element that is placed after a word or word root to make a term of different use or meaning. For example, the suffix *-age* has a general meaning of "belonging to." *Postage* (*post* plus *age*) has to do with a series of stations along a route that receive and send mail. With this sense of *-age* in mind, words such as *coinage, fruitage, bondage,* and *spoilage* become somewhat clearer.

Because they are added to a word or root after meaning has been established, suffixes are usually not so important in word study as are roots and even prefixes. Suffixes can change the meanings of words, but they are primarily used to indicate the functions (uses) of terms. A suffix can, for example, change a singular to a plural: girl, girls. It can indicate the time of action (that is, the tense) of a verb: *talk, talked*.

Suffixes appear primarily to tell us whether a given word is a modifier (adjective or adverb), an action word (verb), or the name of a person or place. In other words, suffixes usually have more general, less specific, meanings than either roots or prefixes, but knowing their approximate meanings is a real aid in building and using a vocabulary.

Among suffixes that may form modifiers can be mentioned "al"—*postal* (belonging to the mails); "ary"—*secondary* (of second rank or influence); and "able"—*peaceable* (peaceful, tranquil). Suffixes such as "ate," "ish," and "ize" often form verbs: *nominate, extinguish, criticize*. The suffix "an" in *American* provides a meaning of "one who lives in America, specifically the United States." The suffixes "ant" and "ent" have related meanings in words such as *inhabitant* (one who lives in a specific place) and *resident* (one who resides).

With this information in mind, give your imagination and knowledge of words a workout. What words can you think of that have the following suffixes? (To help you along, if the prefix were "ly" you would have no trouble thinking of *freely, quickly, smartly, rapidly*, etc.)

-est	-or
-less	-scope
-ate	-es
-meter	-fy
-ence	-ite
-ion	-ar
-ist	-ive
-ory	-cule
-ing	-ine
-able	-ling

Other common suffixes to keep in mind include these:

-ana	Americana, collegiana
-ance	connivance, nonchalance
-dom	kingdom, freedom
-er	loiterer, embezzler
-fold	manifold, twofold
-ful	beautiful, harmful
-graph	monograph, lithograph
-hood	childhood, priesthood
-ice	apprentice, novice
-ish	British, girlish
-ism	barbarism, plagiarism
-ity	civility, nobility
-let	bracelet, ringlet
-like	lifelike, childlike
-logy	trilogy, theology
-ness	kindness, preparedness
-phone	telephone, megaphone
-polis	metropolis, megalopolis
-ship	friendship, statesmanship
-some	twosome, quarrelsome
-ward	toward, afterward
-ways	always, sideways
-wise	clockwise, sidewise
-y	dreamy, infamy

COMBINING FORMS

A *combining form* is a term for a word element that rarely appears independently but forms part of a longer word. *Graph*, for instance, is a combining form (as well as a suffix) that appears in such words as "photograph" and "lithography." *Cardio* appears in a word such as "cardiology." Placed together, *cardio* and *graph* form the word "cardiograph." *Decem*, a combining form with the meaning of "ten," added to the letters "ber," gives us the word "December," the tenth month of the ancient Roman year (which began in March).

Knowing the general meanings of such forms as the following will help in increasing your vocabulary:

anima	life, breath	animal, animation
aqua	water	aquarium, aqualung
aristos	the best	aristocrat, aristocracy
beatus	blessed	beatitude, beatification
bios	life	biosphere, biopsy
causa	cause	causal, causation
culpa	fault	culprit, culpable
domus	house	domestic, domicile
ego	I	egoism, egocentric
facilis	easy	facile, facilitate
gramma	letter	grammar, grammatical
hostis	enemy	hostile, hostility
lex	law	legal, legalize
liber	book	library, libretto
locus	place	local, locality
mater	mother	matriarch, maternal
navis	ship	navy, navigate
opus	work	operation, opera
pedi	foot	pedestrian, pedicure
petra	rock	petroleum, petrology
plus, pluris	more	plural, plurality
populus	people	population, populate
sanctus	holy	sanctuary, sanctify
sophia	wisdom	sophomore, sophisticated
tacitus	silence	tacit, taciturn
thermo	heat	thermometer, thermal
umbra	shade	umbrella, umbrage
vita	life	vital, vitamin

Just to make sure that you are serious about increasing your vocabulary through methods just discussed, work the following exercises. (And don't look at the answers on page 151 until you are stumped or wish to verify your findings.)

1. The word *allow* has several synonyms, among them *let, permit, suffer* and *tolerate*. What synonyms can you think of for *let*.

2. The word *choice* has many synonyms. List at least five.

3. Give one antonym for each of the following: *arrive, atrocious, arrogant, dark, latent, solitary, sophisticated, temporary, weak, wordy.*

4. Give the meaning of each of the following prefixes and list five common words containing each prefix: *bi-, cross-, non-, pre-, sub-.*

5. Give the meaning of each of the following suffixes and list five common words containing each suffix: *-al, -est, -less, -ist, -ment.*

6. With the aid of your dictionary, list as many words as you can that are based on the combining form *centi*, meaning "hundred" or "hundredth."

Building and using an effective vocabulary takes real effort over a long period. But the task can be fun. It can also be rewarding: no better way to a better job has ever been thought of. Give it a try, a real try. And keep on keeping on. Big shots, we're told, were once little shots who kept on shooting.

ANSWERS TO TEST ON PAGE 141

1. clearness
2. look
3. unrelated
4. delay
5. foreign
6. approved
7. destroy
8. unbelieving
9. tiresomely
10. soundness
11. confusion
12. unpremeditated
13. similar
14. tease
15. absorb
16. sleepy
17. prepare
18. powerful
19. appointment
20. top
21. reference
22. clear
23. perilous
24. accused
25. vigor

ANSWERS TO EXERCISES ON PAGE 150

1. *As verb*: abandon, assign, hire out, lease, leave, rent
   As noun: hindrance, impediment, obstacle, obstruction
2. *As noun*: option, selection, preference, election, alternative
   As adj.: exquisite, elegant, rare, delicate, dainty

3. arrive: depart, leave, withdraw, retire
   atrocious: humane, virtuous, noble, genteel, righteous
   arrogant: meek, unassuming, modest, humble, submissive
   dark: light, bright, brilliant, radiant, luminous
   latent: patent, evident, manifest, obvious, apparent, palpable
   solitary: accompanied, attended, escorted, convoyed
   sophisticated: naive, simple, natural, artless, ingenuous
   temporary: permanent, lasting, stable, perpetual, perdurable
   weak: strong, stout, sturdy, tenacious, stalwart
   wordy: concise, terse, succinct, compressed, pithy
4. bi-: two, twice, doubly—biannual, bicameral, bicentennial, bicycle, bilingual
   cross-: going across, counter—crossroad, crossbar, cross-eye, crossbreed, cross-examine
   non-: not—nonabsorbent, nonaggression, nonbreakable, nondescript, nonplus
   pre-: prior to, in advance, early—preschool, prewar, preference, prehistoric, prepaid
   sub-: under, below, secretly—subway, subtract, subversion, substation, sublet
5. -al: of, related to, characterized by—optional, directional, fictional, withdrawal, national
   -est: suffix of the superlative—latest, highest, longest, hardest, luckiest
   -less: destitute of, without—childless, luckless, witless, peerless, countless
   -ist: characteristic of, relating to, one who does—bicyclist, apologist, dramatist, machinist, internist
   -ment: concrete result, means, or instrument—refreshment, embankment, entertainment, amazement, ornament
6. centigrade, centigram, centime, centimeter, centipede, centennial, centurion, centenary, percent, century, centavo, centenarian, centiliter, centillion, centuple.

CHAPTER 20

Straight and Crooked Thinking

Why a chapter on thinking in a book about talking oneself into a better job? Not only that. Why is it placed in the important final position? It's placed here because the author thinks it is the most important single step in your entire campaign.

Reflect on this: when we think, we are talking to ourselves. Every time we tackle a problem we have to talk to ourselves. Every time we plan something, we need to talk to ourselves. For every decision we make, we have to rely on our thoughts. An American writer, Oliver Wendell Holmes, once commented: "A word is the skin of a living thought." If one's thought is without value or is non-existent, all you learn about words and their ways will also be worthless. "We do not think enough about thinking, and much of our confusion is the result of current illusions in regard to it." Thus begins a famous essay, "On Various Kinds of Thinking," by James Harvey Robinson.

Perhaps we do not think enough about thinking because thinking is hard work, because we seem to get along fairly well without doing much of it—possibly because we think we are thinking when actually we are doing nothing of the sort. We are only too ready to ignore, twist, or exaggerate evidence. Some errors in reasoning violate that rare and valuable commodity, plain common sense. Other errors involve logic.

You may consider yourself a rational person and believe that every statement you make is reasonable. If so, think again. Neither you nor I nor anyone else can make every statement fully reasonable because reasoning is based upon facts or what are considered facts. And facts, or assumed facts, change with time. For example, the facts of medicine or physics or population growth or air pollution only a few years ago are hardly the *facts* today. Reasoning is also based upon conclusions drawn from facts; yet the conclusions one reasonable man draws from a given set of facts may differ widely from those of another man.

Clearly, then, you cannot make every statement reasonable. But at least you can avoid making statements that are obviously questionable; and if you do make such a statement, you should be prepared to defend it. You should make your meaning clear by offering evidence. You can usually avoid statements based on faulty premises, those based on false analogy, those involving mere generalizations. How logical, for example, are these statements?

> All motor vehicles should have governors limiting their speed to 50 miles an hour. (What about police cars? ambulances? fire trucks?)
>
> Since football is the most dangerous of all sports, my parents refused to allow me to play it when I was in school. (Overlook the possible parental muddleheadedness: What about water polo? bullfighting? skin diving?)
>
> Steve knows all there is to know about stocks and bonds. (All? Absolutely nothing he doesn't know?)
>
> Gambling is a bad habit; everyone should avoid it because habits are bad. (Can you prove gambling is a bad habit? Are habits bad? all habits? What about the habit of paying your debts? telling the truth?)

You may also believe that you possess a logical mind. Indeed, if you accept a definition of logic as "logical reasoning," you may be partially right. If you agree with this quotation from *Alice's Adventures in Wonderland*, you certainly are right:

> "Contrariwise," continued Tweedledee, "if it was so, it might be; and if it were so, it would be; but if it isn't, it ain't. That's logic."

INDUCTION AND DEDUCTION

It is more likely, however, that you—like all other people—use and abuse two common methods of thinking every day. These methods are *induction* and *deduction*.

The former seeks to establish a general truth, an all-embracing principle or conclusion. The inductive process begins by using observation of specific facts, which it classifies. From a sufficient number of these facts, or particulars, the inductive process leads into a general principle, a comprehensive conclusion. Movement of thought is from the *particular* to the *general*.

Deduction, conversely, tries to show how a particular statement is true because it is part of, and leads down from, a general principle or truth. Movement of thought is from the *general* to the *particular*.

In *inductive* reasoning a set of particulars is studied experimentally and, from observations made, a general principle is drawn or formed. For example: Every horse I have seen has four legs; therefore, I can expect all horses to have four legs. In *deductive* reasoning an accepted general statement, which may be true or false, is applied to a particular situation or case. For example: All horses are animals; this is a horse; therefore, this is an animal.

Processes of thought such as these may seem different from your own thinking processes. Nevertheless, everyone reasons this way. For example, early in history, men became convinced that no one lives forever, that sooner or later all men die. Through inductive thinking, mankind arrived at a general conclusion: "All men are mortal."

A generalization as well established as this, one that needs no further testing, may be used as a starting point, that is, a *premise* in deductive thinking. In light of the general truth that all men are mortal, we examine the future of a man named Ned Weston. This deductive process may be expressed in the form of a *syllogism*.

Major premise:	All men are mortal.
Minor premise:	Ned Weston is a man.
Conclusion:	New Weston is mortal.

Although we do not arrange our thoughts in syllogisms such as the one just illustrated, we reason in much the same way. For example, we assume that events encountered in the future will be like those met with in the past. What, indeed, is the real meaning of the saying, "A burnt child dreads the fire"?

In induction, the possibility of exceptions always exists, but those general conclusions reached by inductive processes are usually acceptable. When you write "most honor graduates of high school do well in college," you cannot be certain because you cannot have examined all records of past and present students and cannot be positive about the future. But the statement is probable. So is the inductive conclusion that no two people have identical fingerprints or footprints, although this statement, too, is only theoretically capable of being positively proved.

Through inductive reasoning, the laws (that is, the principles, the generalized and descriptive statements) of any science, such as chemistry and physics, have been arrived at. Through deductive reasoning they are applied in particular situations: the launching of a space rocket, the manufacture of a computer, the development of a vaccine. In pure and applied science, such reasoning is virtually foolproof. But loopholes do occur where human beings and human behavior are concerned.

Although there are no other ways to think than inductively and deductively, perhaps you want to focus more specifically on the particular errors you might make in thinking. Not only might make—*do* make. For instance, has anyone ever said to you, "That's your opinion, friend, and not a fact"? Is it possible that he or she is correct? Have you confused opinion and fact? When you make a sweeping statement that something or other is a "fact" or is "a sure thing" or is "certain to happen," are you positive of your position? How do you react when someone says that your belief is good so far as it goes but that there are powerful arguments against it? Do you ever make the mistake of thinking that when you give one good reason for something, you have built a solid case? Do you ever provide evidence that applies to what you're saying but that falls far short of real proof?

Is it possible that some belief you have is biased in a particular way because of where you were born or how you were raised? Have you ever delivered yourself of a dogmatic statement about some serious moral or religious issue, overlooking the fact that thousands of highly intelligent people have come to no final conclusion about it?

Everyone is entitled to opinions, but not everyone has developed a flexible mind when talking to himself. If we can learn to talk to ourselves in different ways, that will mean that we have learned to think in different ways. Different ways of thinking and talking will result in a different you—one who may be more likely to get ahead in mind, spirit, and job performance.

LOGICAL LOOPHOLES

The remainder of this chapter briefly discusses the nine most common offenses against straight thinking that most people commit on a daily basis. Study them carefully. Apply each of them to the way you talk to yourself and to others.

1. Hasty generalization

The most prevalent error in inductive reasoning is observing only a few instances and then jumping to a conclusion. For instance, you know a few athletes whom you consider stupid; does it follow that all, or even most, athletes are mentally deficient? What is the specific evidence for labeling certain groups "hippie freaks," "irresponsible women drivers," "dumb blondes," or "male chauvinist pigs"? What is the evidence for "every schoolboy knows . . ." or "all good Americans realize. . . ." or "statistics show. . . ."?

2. Non sequitur

A major error in thinking is the "it does not follow" assumption. *Non sequitur* is an inference or conclusion that does not proceed from the premises or materials upon which it is apparently based. This fallacy can be caused by a false major premise and by a minor premise that is only apparently related to the major premise. For example, some good professional writers admit to being poor spellers. Are you justified in concluding that you, too, also a poor speller, are destined to be a good professional writer? These syllogisms illustrate the *non sequitur* flaw in thinking:

> All members of X club are conceited.
> Frances is not a member of X club.
> Therefore, Frances is not conceited.

> Some members of X club are conceited.
> Frances is a member of X club.
> Therefore, Frances is conceited.

3. Post hoc, ergo propter hoc

A name applied to a variation of hasty generalization, *post hoc, ergo propter hoc* means in English "after this, therefore on account of this." The error it involves is to hold that a happening which precedes another must naturally or necessarily be its cause or that when one event follows another the latter event is the result of the first. "I have a cold today because I got my feet wet yesterday." "No wonder I had bad luck today; I walked under a ladder yesterday." The Roman Empire fell after the birth and spread of Christianity. Would anyone argue that Christianity alone directly caused the fall of Rome? Those who do—and many have—make the *post hoc, ergo propter hoc* mistake in reasoning.

4. Biased or suppressed evidence

Facts that furnish ground for belief and that help to prove an assumption or proposition constitute evidence. An obvious flaw in reasoning is selecting evidence from questionable sources or omitting evidence that runs contrary to the point you wish to make. The testimony of dedicated yoga disciples is in itself not sufficient to prove that practicing yoga promotes a peaceful mind or a healthful, happy life. What do those who do not practice yoga think? What do physicians and philosophers think? other authorities? recent converts? those who once practiced yoga and have given it up?

Figures and statistics can lie if evidence is biased or suppressed. Many of the so-called truths we hear and read have been prepared by paid propagandists and directly interested individuals or groups. Biased and suppressed evidence has caused everyone to recognize that "figures don't lie, but liars figure."

5. Distinguishing fact from opinion

A fact is based on actuality of some sort, a *verifiable* event or statement, whereas opinion is an inference that may be mingled with a supposed fact. That Ernest Hemingway was "an American writer" is a statement that can be proved. That Hemingway was "the greatest American novelist of the twentieth century" is only an opinion of those who hold it. That Thomas Jefferson was President from 1801 until the inauguration of James Madison in 1809 is a fact; that Jefferson was "our greatest President" is a matter of opinion. A favorite device of many speakers is to mingle opinions with facts and thus obscure the difference between them.

6. Begging the question

This flaw in thinking consists of taking a conclusion for granted before it is proved or assuming in the propositions (premises) that which is to be proved in the conclusion. A question as "Should a vicious man like Charles Grundy be allowed to hold office?" is "loaded" because it assumes what needs to be proved. Common forms of begging the question are *slanting, name calling*, and *shifting the meaning of a word*.

Using unfairly suggestive words to create an emotional attitude (as in the application of *vicious* to Charles Grundy, above) is a form of slanting. It is also a form of *argumentum ad hominem*, a Latin phrase loosely translated as meaning "argument against the person." That is, it is an argument against the person who may hold an opinion rather than against the opinion itself: "Only an idiot would believe that."

Guard against using or fully believing such suggestive words and phrases as *bigoted, saintly, progressive, reactionary, un-*

democratic ideas, or *dangerous proposal.* Use them if you have supporting evidence; accept them if the proof offered seems valid. Otherwise, avoid slanting in talking and be on guard when reading and listening.

Name calling is closely allied to slanting. It appeals to prejudice and emotion rather than to the intellect. It employs "good" words to approve and accept, "bad" words to condemn and reject. Be cautious in using such terms as *two-faced, yes man, angel in disguise, rabble rouser, benefactor, do-gooder,* and so on.

Shifting the meaning of a word consists of using the same word several times with a shift in meaning designed to confuse the reader or listener. A *conservative* disposed to preserve existing conditions and to agree with gradual rather than abrupt changes is one thing; a *conservative* unswervingly opposed to all progress, a reactionary, is another. Student *unions* are one thing; labor *unions* are another. Should every citizen vote the Republican ticket because ours is a great *republic*, or vote the Democratic ticket because this a great *democracy*?

7. Evading the issue

This error in logic is most common in heated arguments. It consists of ignoring the point under discussion and making a statement that has no bearing on the argument. If you tell a friend that he drives too fast and he responds that you are a poor driver yourself, he has evaded the issue. He may be right, but he has neither met your objection nor won the argument. Such argument in especially common in political campaigns. It is easy to sidestep an issue and launch a counterattack.

8. Faulty analogy

Because two objects or ideas are alike in one or more respects, they are not necessarily similar in some further way. *Analogy* (partial similarity) can be both accurate and effective; otherwise we could not employ either similes or metaphors. But when we use figurative-language analogy, we do not expect such a figure of speech to *prove* anything.

In the kind of talking most of us do most of the time, an

analogy is chiefly useful as an illustration. In many analogies, differences outweigh similarities. "Why do we need social security? Do we help trees when they lose their leaves in autumn winds? Do we provide assistance to dogs and horses in their old age? Don't some tribes kill people when they are too old to be useful?" Such analogy as this is obviously absurd, but even more literal analogies than this can be ridiculous. You may, for example, reason that since the honor system has worked well in several small colleges, it will work equally well in large universities. Are the similarities between the schools either superficial or less important than the differences? The whipping post was a deterrent to crime in seventeenth-century New England. Is it false analogy to suggest that similar punishment should be inflicted on twentieth-century criminals and dope addicts?

9. Testimonials

Citing statements from historical personages or well-known contemporaries is not necessarily straight thinking. In an attempt to bolster an argument, we are quick to employ such terms as *authorities have concluded, science proves, doctors say, laboratory tests reveal.* George Washington, Thomas Jefferson, and Abraham Lincoln—justly renowned as they are—might not have held economic, social, and political views necessarily valid in the twentieth century. Douglas MacArthur was a great military strategist, but something he said about combustion engines may be less convincing than the words of a good local mechanic. Is an authority in one field an oracle of wisdom about any subject on which he speaks or writes? As a witness for or against an important educational policy, how effective would an eminent surgeon be? a football hero? a TV personality? If you were writing an attack on vaccination, would you reasonably expect the opposition of an opponent to outweigh the pronouncements of the entire medical profession?

But even where there is little question of the validity of authority, be careful to see that neither bias nor the time element weakens your presentation. Some businessmen and labor leaders are experts on economic problems, but their particular interests might prevent their having the impartiality, the objectivity, of a disinterested observer. As for timing, remember that in many fields of human activity and knowledge, authorities soon become obsolete. Charles Darwin no longer has the last word on evolution: Sigmund Freud is not universally considered the last word on psychoanalysis.

How about a short test to find out how well you have understood the contents of this chapter? How would you reply to the following statements? Assign a number to each logical loophole, using the numbers that appear on preceding pages.

1. Lazy workers sometimes get fired. My office mate is the laziest person I have ever met. Therefore, he is going to get fired because of his laziness.
2. Degraded and inhuman as they are, boxing matches must be banned.
3. First student: Is there a relationship between intelligence and high grades? Second student: Let's not discuss the subject. All those who earn high grades are dull, uninteresting persons.
4. Dissecting animals is an evil, wicked practice. How would you like to have your arm, leg or finger snipped off?
5. Books on marriage and the family cannot prepare anyone for marriage. Trying to educate persons for this experience is like trying to teach them to swim without letting them go into the water.
6. The office manager's wife is lovely. But she is a sober-looking woman, and I am convinced she is unhappily married.
7. Oliver Wendell Holmes, Jr., the Supreme Court Justice, was a greater American than his father, the doctor and writer.
8. The prosecution is prepared to prove to you that this depraved murderer who sits before you is guilty as charged.
9. From the instructions I have been given in this office I am prepared to state that all supervisors are hopeless incompetents.
10. In reply to the candidate's claim that his administration is ready to help the poor, I wish to point out that he in-

herited a fortune, has never been hungry, and that his children attend private schools.

Don't peek. But if you want to know what the fallacies are, here are answers corresponding to the *logical loopholes* given in preceding pages: 2, 6, 7, 8, 8, 2, 5, 6, 1, 6.

A final word: don't make the mistake of thinking you're thinking when you aren't. An American humorist once remarked: "If you make people *think* they're thinking, they'll love you. If you make them think, they'll hate you." Crooked thinking is much easier than straight thinking. But since you can't ever say anything at all without some sort of thinking, try to make it the kind that will speed you on your way and not the kind that will hold you back.

Straight thinking makes for straight talking. Because speech is, as the great writer Thomas Mann once said, "civilization itself," it's important that we think straight in order to talk straight and thus get ahead with a career we dream of.

"You should say what you mean," said the March Hare to Alice in Wonderland.
"I do," Alice hastily replied; "at least—I think I mean what I say—that's the same thing, you know."
"Not the same thing a bit!" said the Mad Hatter. "Why, you might as well say 'I see what I eat' is the same thing as 'I eat what I see!' "
Lewis Carroll